THE RESCUE

God's Amazing Grace

OLIVER ALMONARES
with **PHIL FORTUNO**

THE RESCUE
God's Amazing Grace

Military History / Inspirational

Published by MindSpark Publishing in the Republic of the Philippines

This book is dedicated to the heroes of faith who steadfastly fought on the spiritual battlefield with the full armor of God – the belt of truth, the breastplate of righteousness, the shield of faith, the helmet of salvation, the sandals of readiness, and the sword of the Spirit – to rescue those who were captives of sin.

CONTENTS

FOREWORD

Former Philippine Army Scout Ranger Captain Oliver Almonares, the primary character in this book, was on the front lines of the Philippine's war on terror. He and the men of his unit were men of purpose. They were trained to analyze different terrains and determine how to intercept the enemy. He and his men were confident of their capabilities, and they truly cared for each other.

Oliver's intriguing story intersects mine in a unique way. Martin and I were missionaries in the Philippines for 15 years. We were taken hostage by the Abu Sayyaf in 2001. After 376 days of captivity, Martin was killed, but I was freed during a rescue operation. Oliver was the officer-in-charge of the special unit that pressed on during the rain that fateful afternoon. When we talked on that wet hillside just after the rescue, who would have known that years later, we would remain the closest of friends.

I am most appreciative of the Philippine soldiers' efforts to help us during our plight. Many lost their lives during that offensive. Many are still doing so. The mission of the Armed Forces of the Philippines (AFP) was – and continues to be – a noble and worthwhile effort.

This book doesn't end with our rescue, though. The same tenacity that Oliver showed during his Scout Ranger career shows up again and again – as he helped start a church, as he launched a kids' basketball ministry, and as he shares the Gospel in the workplace. It chronicles his move to Canada, and ultimately to the U.S. where our paths cross whenever we can arrange it.

Oliver brings to this book an excellent account of Filipino bravery and resourcefulness. It is also an account of God's leading each step of the way. In each of the seasons in his life, he has learned that "The Battle Belongs to the Lord." He wishes to remain a good soldier of the Cross and continue to give God the glory.

I know that you will enjoy this story. It is an insightful account of soldiering, of ministry, of persevering, and of growth.

Gracia Burnham

INTRODUCTION

"The Rescue: God's Amazing Grace" is a story of self-centered ambitiousness to selfless service, defiance to submission, indifference to love, rot to redemption – a reflection of what had been, what is now and what could be. It focuses on God's sovereignty, not only in the life of former Philippine Army Scout Ranger Captain Oliver Almonares, but also in the lives of those God has placed along his path. The book also chronicles how God redeemed Oliver from a spiritual abyss, and has since used his life's circumstances to work for His honor and glory.

Years ago, in 2002, Oliver and his 15th Scout Ranger *(Mandirigma)* Company successfully rescued Gracia Burnham – an American missionary – after over a year of captivity at the hands of the Abu Sayyaf Group, a band of ruthless terrorists on the island of Mindanao in southern Philippines. The incident would put all of them on a path that would change their lives in ways they never imagined – a transformation they never expected. The rescue would become a significant milestone in the lives of everyone involved in the operation. It would eventually become the invisible umbilical cord that would connect each of them over the years, becoming one of the primary anchors of their lives to this day.

The story highlights the historic rescue from the lenses of the troops involved and its overarching impact on them. The authors know very well that soldiery, or even dying for one's country, does not come naturally. It requires belief in the worthiness of one's cause and the nobility of one's leaders, but is also powered by a faith beyond human understanding. It is a commitment to something spiritual that is most often misunderstood, or outright dismissed, by many. The reflections of the narrators, particularly Oliver, will show and lead the reader to something deeper than what we all easily see on the surface. The experiences of these characters have made them who they are now. With dignity, they have taken all the good and bad events in their lives and turned them into lessons to better themselves. To quote the words of the world-renowned American activist and author Helen Adams Keller, "*Character cannot be developed in ease and quiet. Only through experience of trial and suffering can the soul be strengthened, vision cleared, ambition inspired, and success achieved.*"

The book also honors the selfless sacrifices of the Scout Rangers and other units who took part in all the military operations mentioned. It will give the readers firsthand accounts, not only of the rescue that caught global attention, but also of the lives of soldiers on and off the battlefield. The vivid, action-filled narrative will give readers a peek into the realm of military operations and dreaded scenes of brutal wars. Every soldier and war veteran knows there is always that part in him that remains on the battlefield. It is that part of his life that keeps him connected to the past, particularly to his fallen comrades. Hence, it becomes the duty of the living to pay homage to the people who enriched their past and to all those who never came back to their families alive.

While most people might prefer to look at the world with a 'half-empty glass' mindset and fail to appreciate the power of what is already in front of them, Oliver and his company recognize and cherish the value of their struggles and the greatness that was surprisingly brought out in each other by their shared experiences. They may have struggled in the beginning but in the end, they were left stronger. They decided to give their all to their God over and above being committed to their country, while still with the First Scout Ranger Regiment of the Philippine Army's Special Operations Command. They truly learned what it takes to be a good follower and leader. As for Oliver, he knew well how to command and to selflessly serve – nothing more, nothing less.

This book presents God's supreme power in the mundane activities of man. Battles are not solely won by well-trained warriors, but through the power of prayer to the sovereign Almighty God. We are reminded that life's toughest battles are not just on the battlefields but in the wide arena of everyday life. Man may think he is the captain of his own soul, but in the end, he realizes that God will eventually achieve His own purpose. The Lord said in *Jeremiah 1:5 (NIV):* "Before I formed you in the womb I knew you, before you were born I set you apart." We may not be set apart as prophets like Jeremiah, but this verse reminds us that we all have a purpose in life. Yours may seem trivial, but it is undoubtedly significant in God's economy. A closer and more serious examination of the past helps us make wiser decisions today and tomorrow. So we strive to emulate noble acts of reputable people because if we fail to look and examine our past, we condemn ourselves to make the same kinds of mistakes.

A rescue can be manifested in different forms. One can be rescued physically, emotionally or spiritually. Above all, this book is about a spiritual rescue, made by the greatest rescuer of all time, Jesus Christ. He was the one who sacrificed His life as a ransom for many *(Matthew 20:28, Mark 10:45)*. While soldiers are the instruments of many human rescue missions, it is only Jesus who can truly rescue humankind from eternal damnation and bring them to God's eternal presence. Soldiers may die to win us our physical freedom but only Jesus died to give us eternal life.

In summary – and though the authors do not wish to pontificate – may the reflections and insights herein, encourage us to fulfill our respective life's purposes as we submit to Christ Jesus. May this story give the readers a road map, or a minute idea of how God can be glorified through one's life calling.

•••••

CHAPTER 1

ALL-OUT WAR

"And call upon me in the day of trouble;
I will deliver you, and you shall glorify me."

— Psalm 50:15 (ESV)

Camp Adriano Hernandez
Dingle, Iloilo, Philippines
02 1500H May 2000

"Good afternoon, Rangers!"

It was the voice of my company commander, 1Lt Leroy Daanton, a member of Philippine Military Academy (PMA) *"Maalab"* Class of 1993 and Scout Ranger (SR) Class 114-93. He was addressing the troops of the 15th Scout Ranger (*Mandirigma*) Company – our unit.

The assembled troops responded with a loud synchronized greeting: *"Good afternoon, Sir!"*

1Lt Daanton paused for a while, cleared his throat and then stated, *"Higher Headquarters has given us a few days to prepare for new deployment. We will reinforce our fellow Rangers in Central Mindanao. Our comrades have been fighting it out deep inside enemy territory for several weeks now, and our brother-in-arms, First Lieutenant Jake Paler together with some of his Rangers, gave the ultimate sacrifice for God and country. May*

God bless their souls...Prepare everything we need for combat operations in Mindanao and be ready for the long haul!"

1Lt Daanton's statement caught us by surprise. His announcement was met by solemn silence as we all let the news sink in. Everyone knew who 1Lt Paler and his 18th Scout Ranger *(Makamandag)* Company (18SRC) were. They were fine gentlemen and esteemed brothers.

1Lt Joseph Jake Paler, the commanding officer of the 18SRC, was an outstanding member of Philippine Army's Officer Candidate School (OCS) Class 11-94 and SR Class 122-95. He was one of the well-respected Scout Ranger officers in the First Scout Ranger Regiment (FSRR). *Sir Jake*, as many would call him, was a jolly and grounded young officer who never hesitated to go with the troops wherever and whenever it mattered most. 1Lt Paler was a huge loss to the battle-hardened 18SRC he was leading at that time.

As battle-scarred Scout Rangers, we have heard sad announcements like that before but we never got used to it. The first thing that came to our minds was the grief of the families left behind by the fallen. It also reminded us of what our own families would go through if we got killed. None of us was sacred in the hands of the enemy. We were all fair game as combatants – such is the reality of our profession, and of war.

After a few moments of silence, 1Lt Daanton went on to discuss the details of our upcoming deployment. *"Troops and some essential equipment are the priority. We will be transported by C-130 to Cotabato. But other logistics, together with our M35 truck, will be transported by sea,"* he said. *"Make the necessary preparations. Is there any question? None? You are dismissed!"*

Everyone responded in unison, *"Rangers lead the way! Hooaah!"*

We were anxious and apprehensive. Behind our tough facade, we were simply human. Our hearts were often torn between love of country and love of our respective families. However, we could not let our emotions overwhelm us. It is naturally uncharacteristic to soldiers. We had to keep to ourselves whatever emotions and opinions we may have had. No murmuring, no complaints. There was "business" to be taken care of and we Scout Rangers had to "lead the way – no more, no less". We just had to do what was required of us, what was needed under the situation.

Terror Spree

Looking back, May 2000 could very well have been called an extraordinarily mean season – especially for the country's military and law enforcement personnel. At that time, the nation was still reeling from the latest high-profile abduction done by the Abu Sayyaf Group (ASG). The ASG is a terrorist group primarily made up of those who had broken away from the Moro National Liberation Front (MNLF).

On April 23, six ASG members armed with assault rifles and several rocket-propelled grenades attacked a dive resort in Sipadan Island located in Sabah, Malaysia. The terrorists abducted 21 people – including several foreign tourists – from the resort. They herded the hostages into boats and off they went.

A video released by terrorists on May 6, 2000 showed that the hostages were being held in southern Philippines – in a remote area in Sulu Province.

The ASG's kidnapping spree continued in the succeeding months. It seemed as if they were in some kind of a kidnapping frenzy. In August, negotiations for the release of their hostages started. At some point, Libyan leader Muammar Gaddafi served as mediator.

Meanwhile, in Metro Manila, people became fearful following two blasts in malls. On May 17, 13 people were injured in an explosion at Glorietta 2 in Makati. Then, on May 21, one person was killed and 17 others were injured from a bomb blast in the women's washroom at Cinema 6 of SM Megamall in Mandaluyong City.

At that time, Defense Secretary Orlando Mercado blamed the separatist MILF for the SM Megamall and Glorietta blasts.

A report by *The Philippine Star* on the SM Megamall bomb blast noted: "The worst fighting in Mindanao in recent years erupted last month when the military attacked MILF rebels occupying Secretary Narciso Ramos Highway in Maguindanao. The MILF then threatened to retaliate by attacking cities in Mindanao."

The MILF denied responsibility for the Metro Manila bombings. The Glorietta blast was later attributed to a gang war, but the SM Megamall blast was a different story.

In August 2003, two suspects in the SM Megamall bombing, Dante Ambo and Danny Boisan, were arrested. They were identified as MILF members.

In March 2008, another MILF member named Rahim Buday was arrested for the SM Megamall bombing. Buday was Boisan's cousin. AFP spokesman and Civil Relations Service (CRS) commander Brigadier General Jose Angel Honrado said: "He has admitted his participation to the SM Megamall bombing."

MILF spokesperson Eid Kabalu confirmed that the SM Megamall bombing suspects were indeed MILF members, but he stressed that the group did not sanction any mall bombings.

Nevertheless, the Philippine military faced a very tough challenge. Aside from usual rebel groups, they now had to contend with the so-called breakaway groups who, at times, seemed to be more violent and unpredictable. The ASG certainly belonged in this category. The country's soldiers would go up against the same group of terrorists numerous times. The troops had their awesome victories – but a number of them also lost their lives in the line of duty.

While it is true that soldiers are constantly reminded of death each time they get ready for battle, this reality never gets easier for any of them.

•••

Matanog, Maguindanao, Philippines
07 May 2000

I was the platoon leader of the 15th Scout Ranger Company (15SRC) of the FSRR under the Special Operations Command (SOCOM) of the Philippine Army. Mixed feelings drummed inside my chest. I was excited to be reunited with my buddies-in-arms, and to do together what we had trained for years to do. But I also knew the endless possibilities of the high-risk foray that we were getting involved in.

Being back in Matanog, where I was first deployed in 1995, I was disheartened to see the place decimated by war. It was in ruins. It seemed everything had changed for the worse after I left the town. It hurts me because Matanog had occupied a special place in my heart from the first day I set foot on that land. I had friends there and I came to admire their unique culture. Hence, it was depressing to see the place that was so naturally and culturally beautiful turned to a virtual wasteland by war and random acts of violence. The residents had all either moved to evacuation centers or fled to join their relatives living in safer areas.

What was once a thriving community now bore the devastating landmarks of war – bullet-riddled houses and ground craters created by mortars, cannons, and bombs dropped by planes. The foul smell of dead animals was all over the place, a ghastly place to be in. I felt so sad to see local communities, such as the one in Matanog, deprived of basic life amenities. I couldn't help but ask myself back then, *"Is dignity of human life a strange concept here?"*

Deployments in Mindanao

In September 1995, I was in Matanog for my first combat assignment as a greenhorn second lieutenant. I was assigned as a platoon leader of the 7th Scout Ranger Company under Cpt Corleto Vinluan, a member of PMA "*Maringal*" Class of 1988 and SR Class 100-89. He would later become the Commanding General of the Light Reaction Regiment (LRR) which is also under the SOCOM of the Philippine Army. The LRR is a unit of the Philippine Army that specializes in counterterrorism and urban warfare. In a nutshell, it can be likened to the U.S. Army Delta Force.

Back then, we were operating under Task Group Panther (TGP) commanded by Major Hernando DCA Iriberri, a member of PMA "*Matikas*" Class of 1983 and SR Class 52-83, who went on to become the 56th commanding general of the Philippine Army in 2014. He was subsequently promoted as the 46th Chief of Staff of the Armed Forces of the Philippines (AFP). At the time, we were mostly in the defensive position as the peace talks between the government and the Moro Islamic Liberation Front (MILF) were ongoing. The MILF's armed component, the Bangsamoro Islamic Armed Forces (BIAF), was deemed a serious threat to the peace and security in the area. So, to keep the relative peace in place, troops were deployed and utilized as a deterrent to any hostility between the opposing parties. But still, the atmosphere was tenuous. Both sides, I believe, were suspicious of each other all the time.

When I came back to Maguindanao for my second deployment in year 2000, I was with the 2nd Scout Ranger (*Second to None*) Battalion (2SRB) under the command of Lt Col Noel Coballes, a member of PMA "*Mapitagan*" Class of 1980 and SR Class 33-80. He is a well-decorated Scout Ranger officer who later became the 55th commanding general of the Philippine Army in 2013. He was succeeded by General Hernando DCA Iriberri. In hindsight, I find it quite amazing that my two former commanders in the same combat zone both became commanding generals of the Philippine Army.

Looking back, they were tough field commanders and I learned a lot from them. Knowing their combat exploits, they were the commanders one would not want to fight against on the battlefield.

The lessons I learned not only from my previous commanders but also from other senior officers and colleagues contributed to shaping my professional ethos and leadership philosophy. They had an immense influence on me as a fighting soldier, even after leaving the military service. The discipline at work and tenacity in challenging situations were values that fueled me to be consistent in everything I do and to always persevere.

•••

Matanog, Maguindanao
14 May 2000

It was our seventh day in the battle zone. We were right smack in the middle of the ongoing all-out war declared by then President Joseph Ejercito Estrada against the MILF – a secessionist group that has been fighting for self-determination in some areas in Mindanao. The war was steadily grinding into a bloody and destructive one as casualties rose and villages were abandoned. In a war like this, nobody wins. The entire country practically loses as communities are plunged deeper into poverty and violence.

We started our movement very early that morning. We did not even have time for a meal. In Scout Ranger-type operations, one must always make do with whatever amount of time he has because when it's time to move, everybody moves. Nobody can opt out on the basis of a simple necessity because everything is labeled as "simple" in the field.

The order of movement had 15SRC in the lead. Then, it would be:

- 17SRC led by 1Lt Montano Almodovar, a member of PMA *"Bantay-Laya"* Class of 1994 and SR 121-95, and his Executive Officer, 2Lt Napoleon Agoncillo, a member of PMA *"Kalasag-Lahi"* of 1997 and SR Class 135-99;
- 8SRC under 1Lt Michael Banua – a classmate of 1Lt Daanton in PMA and in SR training;
- 2SRB Command Group of Lt Col Coballes and Cpt Freddie Dela Cruz, the Executive Officer / Operations Officer of 2SRB, who is a member of PMA *"Tanglaw-Diwa"* Class of 1992 and SR Class 107-92;
- 2SRC led by the late 1Lt Ted Tuibuen, an exemplary graduate of the Philippine Army's Officer Preparatory Course (OPC) and SR Class 110-93; and his Executive Officer, 1Lt Marianito De Joya – a classmate of the late 1Lt Jake Paler in OCS and a member of SR Class 125-96; and
- 18SRC, led by my PMA classmate 1Lt Laurence Somera and who is a member of SR Class 125-96 and his Executive Officer, 1Lt Jeffrey Cauguiran, a member of PMA *"Mabikas"* Class of 1996 and SR Class 131-97.

We moved cautiously the whole morning as we crossed creeks and passed through many concrete bunkers. Tactically clearing those fortresses was tedious. We had to be careful, in case the enemy planted landmines and improvised explosive devices (IEDs) along our line of advance (LOA).

There is no room for mistakes on the battlefield. Carelessness or stupidity can easily send one to kingdom come in an instant.

We utilized a movement called "bounding over-watch" whenever the terrain allowed it. It is a military movement technique of alternating movement between units or teams with precise coordination. As one team moves, the other teams take an over-watch posture to secure the one on the move. The teams switch roles as they move forward particularly in areas considered dangerous, or risky for the troops. It was already 11:30 A.M. when we got to the top of a steep hill. That was when I saw the leading team, under Ranger Venancio Tagsip Jr. – a member of SR Class 106-92 - in fighting stance and doing hand signals. Enemy fighters had been sighted!

Seeing my lead team, I quickly moved up front to the position of the team leader. It is standard operating procedure (SOP) for us Scout Ranger commanders to, *"Always lead from the front and be in the thick of the action when shit hits the fan!"*

What I saw was a sizable number of enemy fighters in a huddle. But in an instant, they took a fighting formation. One of them noticed us!

The atmosphere suddenly became tense. *"This is it! This is a huge and messy fight,"* I said to myself.

Wasting no time, I gave commands through hand signals and everybody moved to take their combat positions. Scout Rangers are trained to do combat maneuvers stealthily and silently. Every troop readied for the impending brawl, taking their own stand. Everyone was on edge – and the moment seemed to last for eternity.

My radioman gave me the handset to relay the situation to my Company Commander, who was tactically positioned in the middle of our formation at that time, as we were the leading company of 2SRB. Being in the middle of the pack up-front is the most tactically-sound position of a battlefield commander as he can easily see the front and control his troops right from the center of it all.

Four more Scout Ranger companies were behind us, completing the entire 2SRB. Moving alongside us was a Marine Battalion Landing Team (MBLT) of the Philippine Marines spearheaded by their elite unit, the Marine Corps Force Recon (MCFR).

Then, just 200 meters in front of us were more or less 80 BIAF fighters, who were apparently expecting us, all ready to pound us to pieces! I knew there were even more of them waiting to tear us apart.

Using the sparse vegetation as concealment and coconut trees as cover, we took our fighting positions. The enemy fighters were doing the same thing. They maneuvered forward by moving from one coconut tree to the other towards our positions. They knew we were there, and they were raring to meet us head on! My heart was pounding so hard and fast. I could almost hear its rapid beats. I knew death and destruction was certain in a few moments. We held our breaths as we fixed the front sights of our rifles for the dreaded bloody gun battle that would soon ensue.

My Scout Rangers were already in their skirmisher positions and were ready to pull their triggers once I gave the order. They were raring to mix it up with the enemy. The troops knew it was best to be on the offensive and never on the defensive.

The enemy kept moving forward and they seemed fearless to us. We took our fighting positions. There was no turning back now. My troops knew fully well that we would not give an inch to the enemy. We would fight to the end, and we would honorably fall where we stand – if need be.

The die was cast. We had crossed the Rubicon. There was no turning back the clock, and no time to hesitate. To do otherwise would likely spell the worst tragedy for us.

When the enemy was less than 50 meters away from us, I finally gave the order, *"Fire!"* while pulling the trigger of my rifle in that split second.

---

[1] I prefer to call my troops individually as "Ranger" – aside from calling them "Brother" or "Buddy" – instead of their military rank. To me, "Ranger" isn't only a military specialization but a term of endearment for someone whom I had worked with in actual combat, and had been with during the worst times in my military life.

Boom! Brrrttt! Kablamm! Boom! Brrrrttttt!

All hell broke loose!

It was like Chinese New Year celebrations when all firecrackers were set off to drive bad spirits away and spare everyone from misfortune. It was the worst kind of symphony with an uncoordinated orchestra playing every musician's piece with its own beat and tempo. There was nothing but eerie noise produced by deadly weapons of lethal rounds, mortars, grenades, and what-not.

One can easily be disoriented by the deafening exchange of gunfire, grenade explosions, shouting, and battle cries from both camps. We heard enemy fighters shouting *"Allahu Akbar! Allahu Akbar!"* ["God is great! God is great!"] as they continued to fire at us.

Everyone was in for the brutal fight. I knew it was all or nothing for my troops. To be unforgiving and ruthless in every firefight is one of my standing orders – no compromises. After all, there is no second place in combat. All second placers in combat end up either seriously wounded or dead.

Each man was raring to get his hands first on the enemy's throat. Somebody has to pay the price, and it should be the enemy. For us Scout Rangers, winning in combat – where life is at stake – is non-negotiable. We were trained to win battles at all cost.

After about ten minutes of intense gun battle, I heard my radioman, Ranger Rodolfo Papillera Jr., a member of SR Class 135-99, moaning as tears rolled down from his eyes. He was badly hit and was cringing in serious pain! I could see the soil splattering and debris hitting me as enemy snipers' and machine gun fires reached our position. In a hushed tone, I told him, *"Lipat ka sa kanan!* [Move to the right!]" I encouraged him to move as I saw the barrage of bullets hitting the left side of his position. Patches of soil flew as enemy bullets rained a few inches from his position. He did his best to move but he couldn't. He was grimacing in pain. He yelled, *"Hindi ako makagalaw, sir! Tinamaan ako sa likod, sir!* [I can't move, sir! I got hit it in my back, sir!]"

I knew it was really bad. There was no denying it, but I could not simply tell him lest he lose faith in his chance of surviving the horror.

Then all of a sudden, I felt something hit my left shoulder. I shrugged it off, but a biting pain followed after a few seconds. Still, I tried to disregard it. My focus was on the raging firefight we were in. I need to ably lead my troops. There was nothing that could needlessly occupy my mind, nothing more important than to excellently lead my men in battle.

Several minutes passed, after which I felt a stinging and excruciating pain as my blood oozed and soaked my battle uniform. I felt my warm blood flowing on the skin of my torso.

Damn!

Reality set in. *"This is it. I was hit and it was bad!"* I was bleeding profusely. It was time to face the horrors of another brutal exercise.

But as quickly as the blood flowed out of my body, I kept giving orders to my troops and firing back at the rushing enemy fighters. It was like a nightmare fighting those fierce *mujahideens*, as they labeled themselves. I was horrified to see them stand up after being shot. It could be the unexplained rush of adrenaline of a man with a death wish that kept them going. So, we kept on hitting them as much as we could to totally neutralize them. We learned later that they were using methamphetamine hydrochloride (an illicit drug that is commonly known by its street name *"shabu"*), as evidenced by the drug paraphernalia the troops recovered after the encounter.

Simultaneously, I was giving updates to Lt Col Coballes, my battalion commander, and to 1Lt Daanton, my company commander, as I struggled with my wound, and led my men in battle. My commanders who were in different positions needed updates from me so they could assess and make accurate decisions for the entire 2SRB contingent under the circumstances. They had limited visual as to the size of the enemy unit my troops and I were viciously engaging with up close. Further worsening the situation, we were having problems with communication as our decades-old radios got hit by enemy rounds and began to falter in the heat of battle. As the gun battle became intense and seriously disorienting, reliable radio communication was a serious necessity.

As I was trying to grab the radio handset from my wounded radioman, *Zing!* An enemy bullet hit the left temporal part of his head. His brains splattered on my face!

Oh God!

I was horrified as I looked at his deformed skull soaked in warm blood! Looking at his eyes, I knew he was gone the moment he was hit.

Damn!

My dependable radioman was dead. I was so mad at the sight of him in a pool of his own blood. I could not simply see him that way. He was a good soldier whom I never had any problems with when it came to military discipline and conduct. In fact, he was always ready to lend a helping hand to anyone who needed assistance. That day – May 14 – was his birthday. He was only 24 years old, and he was my good buddy!

Thoughts raced through my mind. I needed to be extremely focused. I had to steel myself in order to survive and get my troops out of the rut.

Amid the raging firefight, several of my men attempted to pull me out from the enemy's firing line. Unfortunately, every time my troops tried to get closer to me, the enemy would deliver a barrage of deadly fire resulting in more casualties on our side. The enemy was cunning. They knew they had a wounded officer in their iron sights and that my troops would certainly rescue me – or recover my dead body, if it had come to that point. The enemy was banking on the fact that whoever attempted to get me out of trouble would get hit 99.99%.

Son of a gun!

Lethal rounds, after all, are never personal. They are indiscriminate, and were generally labeled, "To Whom This May Concern!" Hence, when they head your way, better get the hell out fast because they certainly won't give a damn who you are.

End of the Road?

Lying prostrate on that forsaken spot on that battlefield, I realized I was at my most helpless point. The enemy wasn't giving me any quarter. No mercy – they very well understood that word. They would let me die slowly in pain on that patch of land where I lay bleeding.

It seemed like nobody could pull me out of my position anymore. *"My comrades have given up,"* I thought. I could understand as I didn't want more casualties on our side. I accepted my fate, waiting for the final bullet to take me to eternity. I readied myself. I knew it had been a good fight, and I did all that I could. I would die with my boots on, and with honor.

I started to recall God's goodness, grace, and mercy in my life. I started praying for God not to save my life but to forgive me for not living my life for His honor and glory. After all that was the main purpose why I was created. Though I thought of Him as my Savior, I did not live at that time as if He was my Lord. Yes, I had serious spiritual issues with trusting and obeying.

I accepted my lot. I thought, *"Perhaps my life and purpose just end here. Let me die in battle then."*

But suddenly, memories of my lovely wife and daughter flashed through my mind. My daughter Bea was barely two years old at that time. I imagined her calling me, *"Papa! Papa!"* while I chased her around our small house in Iloilo. I also missed my lovely wife Ena. I remembered our time together, albeit limited – the loud laughs, the funny and restrained public displays of affection whenever we were together. Oh, I seldom see my Ena and Bea! I have missed a lot of important family time with them, all in the name of duty, honor, and service to country. The nature of my profession brought me to many war-torn places and I have been away from my wife and daughter for most of our family life. Have I been fair to my family all this time? Have I been a good husband and father? Above all, have I been a good steward of what God has given me? Have I been a good witness for Jesus?

Tears started rolling down my cheeks. Despite my hesitation, I blurted out, *"Lord, please give me a chance – a chance to make up for my shortcomings to my family and a chance to make it right with you, and serve you."* That was all I could mutter, and then I slowly closed my eyes readying myself for that one final bullet to my head at any moment. My last wish was for my death to be quick and painless, if and when the final bullet hit me.

God's Hands

Out of nowhere, I felt a hand pulling the back of my uniform, dragging me towards the safe zone. Was I hallucinating already? I thought it must be part of the natural thought processes of a dying person. At any rate, I didn't care as long as I physically got out of that sure-death sorry-position I was in!

In my half-conscious state, I saw my comrades, Rangers Ronnie Catague – a member of SR Class 143-01 and Elmo Colorado – a member of SR Class 121-95, fearlessly and roughly pulling me out of the kill zone. They were able to close in to my position amid a hail of deadly enemy gun fires. They were dragging me and at times, were pushing me. Audacity at its finest. They were relentless, they would stop at nothing to rescue me from certain death. They were crazy-brave! But by their unbelievable tenacity, we were able to finally crawl out of the immediate enemy kill zone and they were able to carry me towards our safe zone. I knew in my heart that it was God's hand at work. He uses people for good. That time, He tapped my fellow Rangers to save me from serious physical harm or death.

The gun battle continued. It was unrelenting and unforgiving in its intensity. I was very dizzy due to blood loss. My world was spinning and the pain was excruciating despite the adrenaline rush of the moment. They tried to tie a bandanna around my shoulder to stop the bleeding. My wounded left arm was dangling since I already lost control of it. Worse, we had no medic team present! I had to endure the pain until I could be medically evacuated. But all the time I was thinking, *"I will survive my wounds but I might not be able to play competitive basketball again. Well, at least I can still shoot the ball with my good arm. Thank God!"*

After more or less three hours, which seemed like an eternity, the firefight and gun fire became sporadic and rescue helicopters were eventually on their way to pick us up. Three of my gallant troops – Ranger Rudy Bacyadan (SR Class 135-99), Ranger Danilo Cabical, Ranger Rodolfo Papillera Jr. – and one from the Philippine Marines made the ultimate sacrifice while several of us were wounded.

•••

After almost six hours of pain and blood loss, I was finally ushered to a UH-1H Helicopter. As I listened to the loud choppy sound of the helicopter blades, I gazed at the lifeless bodies covered with Army ponchos at my feet. It was a humbling moment for me. I realized that I was not Superman and that I was expendable – we all were.

I felt my heart being torn apart slowly as I stared blankly at my troops' dead bodies on the floor of the helicopter. They were my brave brothers-in-arms – they were heroes! I closed my eyes and tears quickly rolled down. My heart was heavy. It was wailing loudly for all my buddies, both the killed and the wounded.

Though I was in serious pain, I was able to mumble, *"Thank you, Lord."* The near-death experience truly humbled me. Thoughts flashed through my mind. God was calling my attention to some things. I needed to be grateful, and examine my purpose and significance in life. Did I have a purpose? Definitely I did! I just needed to listen to His voice! I had to be humble.

> "What is man that you are mindful of him, the son of man that you care for him? You made him a little lower than the heavenly beings and crowned him with glory and honor." *Psalms 8:4 to 5 (ESV)*

In his English Standard Version (ESV) Study Bible commentary about the foregoing verse, Dr. John MacArthur stated, "If the whole universe is diminutive in the sight of the Divine Creator, how much less is the significance of mankind. Yet, God made man significant. He was created in the image and likeness of God to exercise dominion over the rest of the creation" (cf. *Genesis 1:26-28*).

Live to Fight Another Day

I was so worn out from too much blood loss, combat fatigue, and mixed emotions. I closed my eyes as we headed to the nearest military hospital in Camp Siongco, home of the 6th Infantry (*Kampilan*) Division of the Philippine Army in Awang, Maguindanao.

Amid the chaos and my roller coaster ride between life and death, I didn't inform my family of what had happened until after the surgery was successful. The military doctor on duty gave me three pieces of metal he had taken from my shoulder.

He explained that the bullet must have hit a hard object like a rock or stone and ricocheted to my shoulder. As a result of debridement, the majority of my deltoid muscle was removed, thus creating a concave-like area on my shoulder.

It was tough to be confined at the hospital. However, I was still thankful that I was so blessed.

Aside from my family, there were other meaningful endeavors that gave me some comfort. Before we were deployed in Matanog, Maguindanao, I was in Iloilo. I had been training and coaching a basketball team made up of kids aged 13 and younger. I remembered they were playing their championship game when I was on my second day at the hospital. In fact, I was able to coach my team via cellphone and we won the championship. Imagine that! That simple achievement reinforced my thinking that *"I'm the man!"* – when in fact it's all God's grace. How shameful it was for me to claim glory that was beyond me!

After a few days, one of my soldiers handed me my newly washed uniform. The left shoulder sleeve of my upper battle dress was torn and ripped. My wornout lousy cap had three bullet holes on its sides. It gave me goose bumps to realize how close those bullets were to my skull. *"Close hits,"* I whispered while I shook my head in disbelief. I felt intense emotions – pride, shame, horror, and gratitude all rolled into one. I was overwhelmed by emotion so I just closed my teary eyes. Truly, God had great plans for me for extending His grace on this side of eternity. Amazing grace!

•••

I recuperated for about a month. My shoulder healed fast and well, but my left arm needed rehabilitation. It had lost some of its strength and function. I also felt terrible pain each time I moved it, preventing me from using it fully. Consequently, it atrophied due to lack of use and activity.

I tried shooting hoops with one hand. It was a humbling moment. "Basketball is life" to me, so I struggled at the thought of being classified as a person with disability (PWD), or worse yet, that I would never get to play basketball ever again. I was terrified at that prospect.

The road to full recovery was worrisome. I felt that if I failed to recover fully, I would be useless – a Scout Ranger who is not, or cannot be, operationally active. That fearful possibility slowly built up inside me. I simply could not accept it. Defeat in any way was unacceptable to me.

The government gave me 20,000 PHP – or the equivalent 385 USD at that time – to help with my rehabilitation expenses. Practically and obviously, it was not enough. But I understood fully the true essence of the word "service." Service might mean that we do not get much financial support when we get hurt in the line of duty. But we nevertheless offer our whole life to fight for our country from all enemies – foreign and domestic. We do what we do so that others may live in peace, and I fully accept the worthiness of it. I had chosen a truly difficult but noble profession.

Battling PTSD

After I celebrated my 30th birthday in July 2000, I reported back to my unit, 15SRC. By then, they were operating in Bohol – an island province in Central Visayas – after a 3-month stint in Maguindanao. Whenever we were brought to a new operational area, we lightheartedly called it our "new playground." Taking every deployment lightheartedly helped us cope quickly with new challenges in the different areas where we had been.

In Bohol, the first thing I did was to look for a basketball court. Finding a spot where we can play basketball had always been one of my top priorities whenever we were deployed in a new area. Oftentimes, it was either I found one or I built one. The nearest we could get was few kilometers away. I was challenged to find a means to satisfy our collective desire to play basketball.

After several weeks, I was able to talk to the road grader operator. I convinced him to flatten the open ground right in front of our barracks. We bought some plywood to make our backboard, and *voila* we had a "state of the art" basketball court! It may have been petty, or even funny, but that makeshift basketball court made a lot of difference in coping with our loneliness, managing the doldrums, and keeping our sanity.

During that time, I was also going through a lot emotionally. I didn't have any idea I was having symptoms of Post Traumatic Stress Disorder (PTSD). Back in those days in the Philippine Army, we never had psychological debriefing to recover from the trauma of combat. I had no way of knowing for sure that I already had severe PTSD. As days passed, I just did my best to cope with pent up emotions and unprocessed traumas. We drowned ourselves with alcohol and other merrymaking pursuits during lulls in combat operations. But in reality, I was seriously suffering inside and my family suffered along with me. There were nights at home during vacation when I would scream while asleep in the middle of the night, *"Maneuver right!"*, or sometimes, *"Assault!"* My wife would wake me up and comfort me. But I always did my best to compose myself and maintain a facade of being in control at all times.

It was painful to me knowing I brought "my war" to our home – to my own family – and it was very unfair to them. I became more reclusive, rarely engaging in typical conversation. They were not used to seeing me like that. I knew they were seriously bothered by what I was becoming in those times. My demeanor gravely affected them. On hindsight, I really feel bad and sorry for the pain I caused my family, relatives, friends and colleagues, in my years of battling PTSD.

•••

Two weeks after I reported back to my unit, we had a combat encounter. This time, it was against the New People's Army (NPA), the armed wing of the Communist Party of the Philippines (CPP). It was not as bloody as the one in Matanog two months earlier.

We made a hasty raid at 3:30   against 20 local communist terrorists based on an intelligence report from one of our deep penetration agents (DPA). We ran through two kilometers of rice fields because there was no access for our "civilian-look transportation." Running in complete combat gear was one of the best applications of our SR training in endurance.

Fighting against the local communist-terrorists required more than just audacity. We had to make timely and cunning raids to really corner them because they can easily mix with the civilian populace or extricate themselves quickly. It was very challenging. It was not one of our best combat experiences, but I won't go much into details. It may not sound modest, but that experience was treated just as a normal SR operation. Nobody died on either side but we recovered a lot of ammunitions and other materials from the enemy that were of high combat-intelligence value.

With that armed encounter, I knew I was back to my natural self and my own habitat – warfighting. I was "home" again.

To keep up with the demands of my high-intensity profession, I simply swept my PTSD under the rug. I became emotionally numb. I kept it to myself. I thought I was just doing a noble thing – never burdening anyone with whatever personal struggles I might have. I was being the quintessential obedient soldier who can always march to hell and back without any complaint or drama. My life as a Scout Ranger, as a warrior, continued.

> "We strike, we who are happy and free. Birds of same feather we flutter together. Scout Rangers of fortune are we. We sing! Greeting the night with a song. Laughing at danger, we fight like a panther and conquer the hardships always…" – *Selected lines of the "Scout Ranger Song"*

Yes, we Scout Rangers are trained to fight like wild panthers – silent, swift, and fearless in battle. But we are also human and we have emotions. We get physically hurt too just like everyone else. I needed a lot of grace. And even more as the days passed.

"He giveth more grace when the burdens grow greater...
He giveth, and giveth, and giveth again." – *Lyrics from
"He Giveth More Grace" by Annie Johnson Flint*

•••••

Morning Talk. Giving words of encouragement after morning exercise. Daily road run and "Army Dozen" exercises were routine part of our Scout Ranger activities to start the day. (ca. 1999)

Marksmanship Training. Regular Marksmanship Training is a must for us to be effective in combat. (ca. 1999)

Officers of the 2nd Scout Ranger Battalion who finished the fight after I was wounded in action.

(L–R) 1Lt Laurence Somera, 1Lt Leroy Daanton, 1Lt Marianito de Joya, 1Lt Montano Almodovar, 1Lt Ted Tuibuen, 2Lt Napoleon Agoncillo, 1Lt Michael Banua, 1Lt Jeffrey Cauguiran.

Officers of the 2nd Scout Ranger Battalion. Lt Col Noel Coballes (third from the left), the Battalion Commander, and Cpt Freddie Dela Cruz (fifth from the left), the Executive Officer of 2SRB.

Close Hit. My Battle Dress Attire (BDA) ripped by the bullet that hit my shoulder.

Top of the World. Taking a rest on top of a mountain after a long day of hunting the enemy.

Some of the troops of the 15th Scout Ranger (*Mandirigma*) Company, under the leadership of Cpt Oliver Almonares. Photo taken at their Company Command Post in Brgy. Cabunbata, Isabela, Basilan (2002).

CHAPTER 2

HUMBLE BEGINNINGS

"Many are the plans in the mind of a man, but it is the
purpose of the LORD that will stand."

— Proverbs 19:21 (ESV)

I was born and raised in the municipality of Alimodian, Iloilo,
a province in the island of Panay. I am the youngest of eight
children of the late Fabian Rodriguez Almonares and Virginia
Demoni Almonares. Ours was a Christian home and we followed
the teachings of the Holy Bible. I came to the saving knowledge
of Jesus Christ when I was eleven years old. I accepted Him as
my personal Savior during the Summer Vacation Bible School
in 1982. However, following His lordship became an issue to
me. A true believer can fully relate to where I was at that time.

My family regularly hosted all Saturday Schools and Vacation
Bible Schools conducted by our local church, which was located
a few kilometers from our village. In all the Vacation Bible
Schools I attended, I always got all the awards. Yes, they gave
awards! Someone even told my mother, *"Maybe Bhoy will be a
preacher or a pastor someday."*

Years later, much to my parents' dismay, I became more of a
"Born Against" rather than a "Born Again" believer. As a child
though, I remember that we always had a lot of things to do during
my Vacation Bible School days. It seemed like everything was
in motion. I was caught up in the flurry of whatever activities

we had. After all, I was a kid who simply loved to hang out and play with other kids. My childhood was mostly spent in church-related activities and I have good memories of them.

In 2008, after more than 30 years of planting the seeds of faith in our village, God allowed us to have the opportunity to be instruments and take the lead in starting a church ministry. But I'll tell you more about that later in this book. It just proves that it's truly amazing how God works in mysterious ways!

The 1980s ushered in a major turning point in the country's more recent history. For one, the People Power Revolution of 1986 – whose focal point was the large crowd that gathered at Epifanio de los Santos Avenue or EDSA – put the world's spotlight on the Philippines. It marked the end of the rule of President Ferdinand Marcos, who had been in office since 1965 and had put the country under Martial Law in 1972. He was ousted and replaced by President Corazon "Cory" Aquino.

With this, many Filipinos hoped for drastic changes to fix the system-wide woes that plagued the Philippine government. Alas, it would turn out years later that this was not the so-called cure-all that everyone was hoping for. The warring political factions of the country never really made their peace with each other.

However, at that time, the nation's euphoria was understandable. The whole world had feted it for the so-called "bloodless revolution." To come of age during this period of great change was both exhilarating and frightening.

Growing up, I struggled with my faith. There were traumatic experiences that affected my perspective. I endured physical, verbal, and psychological abuse from one of our family members. He abused alcohol and when he got drunk, he got very violent. The whole family suffered. I had no definite explanation why those things happened at that time. I was just very confused. We were supposed to be a family taking care of each other.

I know now that turning to alcohol was a cry for help. Unfortunately, back then, my family didn't really know how to deal with it. We did not have support groups like what we have today. We never even discussed it. Perhaps, we kept quiet because of shame, or we simply didn't know how to properly deal with it – the latter reason being the most likely.

My mother was known to be a godly woman while my father was the chief of the village and a deacon in our church. However, as a family, it was as if we were in the wilderness or out in the storm. We had declared our faith in Jesus Christ, yet we were in such a horrible mess. Still, it was God's faithfulness that got us through.

The situation had quite an impact on how I viewed life, particularly bullying. "The bullied eventually become a bully as well – and could even be worse than the original bully." I came up with my own idea of how to be a man. I thought I should be tough and never let anyone walk all over me. That was a very dangerous road to take, but I went there anyway. I wanted to take matters into my own hands. I sought "instant justice." I thought that was the just and most practical way for me to survive in a not-so-ideal world. Thus, I became very defensive, tough, and aggressive as I dealt with everyday challenges. With my tough demeanor, I felt I was becoming *somebody* in our neighborhood who commanded respect. In reality, I was steadily turning into a *hardass* who was secretly despised by my peers.

Despite my mother's best efforts, I found it difficult to integrate into my new-found strategy of being tough with "the fruits of the spirit" mentioned in *Galatians 5:22-23*: *"love, joy, peace, patience, kindness, goodness, faithfulness, gentleness, and self control."*

My mother, the ever loving and patient person that she is, kept on reminding my siblings and me of these "fruits." From the time I was about four or five years old, I could vividly recall my mother listening to a Bible radio program called *Tinapay*

Sang Kabuhi (Bread of Life). She listened attentively with her Bible open and she even made notes. Now, I realized how her faithfulness to the Lord Almighty impacted our lives.

Back then, I kept wondering what motivated her to do it almost every day. She tried her very best to teach us what she knew. She gathered us every night for devotionals, reading the Bible, and singing hymns. She really led us to the right path.

> "Train up a child in the way he should go, and when he is old, he will not depart from it." *Proverbs 22:6 (KJV)*

Dr. Michael Rydelnik and Dr. Michael Vanlaningham explained in The Moody Bible commentary, "This is a proverb, and proverbs describe the common experiences of God's people over long periods of time. Typically, a child whose parents dedicate him to the right path through careful training will continue in that way to old age. This proverb does not treat children mechanistically as if a child cannot walk away from the faith, nor does it assume that humans can force God's hand. Other factors outside parental control may affect outcomes as well. But this proverb stresses 'parental opportunity and duty', encouraging parents to do their part by raising their children well. Even parents of children who may become prodigal can have real hope that when he is old he will not depart from what he has been taught as a child."

I thank God for giving me godly parents. I take responsibility for all the poor and wrong choices that I made. My parents had nothing to do with them.

Now I realize the importance of the values that my father and mother consistently inculcated in us. I may have been off the right path many times, but by God's amazing grace, I am drawn to the value of "reverence to God." The New Living Translation paraphrased *Proverbs 9:10* this way: "Fear of the Lord is the foundation of wisdom. Knowledge of the Holy One results in good judgment."

When we got our first black-and-white television in 1979, people in the village came to our house to watch this great technological wonder. They patiently waited for us to finish our devotions just so they could watch TV, which was a rare commodity in our village back in those days. It was only years later that I realized how God had put us in a great position to be instruments for His glory. The television was His instrument for those people so that they could hear His words through Bible reading and hymns. I have no idea what impact those devotions had on them. But I do know that God said in *Isaiah 55:11 (ESV),*

> "So shall my word be that goes out from my mouth; it shall not return to me empty, it shall accomplish that which I purpose, and shall succeed in the thing for which I sent it."

In spite of the Biblical way they brought us up, my parents had no idea that I was turning out to be the opposite of what they thought I should be. I wanted to be tough and, of course, I was convinced that meant not turning the other cheek. It seemed like being "tough" was my security blanket to counter the challenging environment and situations of my younger years. I decided to be tough instead of fully trusting God through Jesus Christ, my Lord and Savior. In my naïve mind, toughness was the way to handle this physical world. Spiritual fortitude played no part.

I intentionally shunned Christian youth groups. I felt that I would be seen as "weak" if I joined them. It would put me in a very vulnerable position. I also lived a very hedonistic lifestyle. I learned to drink and abuse alcohol in order to gain the approval of the wrong kind of "friends." Ironically, I was becoming the kind of person I had detested. I was losing the very purpose of why I was created by God.

Taming the Wild Tendencies

I was sent by my parents to a private high school in Iloilo City called Central Philippine University Development High School

(CPU-DHS). CPU is known as a private research university in Iloilo City, Philippines. It was established in 1905 through a grant given by the American business magnate, industrialist and philanthropist John D. Rockefeller under the auspices of American Baptist Foreign Mission Society. It is the first Baptist school and second American university in the Philippines and in Asia after Silliman University in Dumaguete City, Negros Oriental, Philippines.

For a poor family like ours, it was a huge financial sacrifice to send me to CPU. My education caused my family to scrimp on our other needs. But my parents, who wanted me to get a good education, would not settle for less. They were determined to send me to the best local school they could afford even with their meager income.

CPU, with its deep Christian doctrine and values, tamed my wild tendencies a bit. There were a lot of "city boys" who were bullies and a "rural kid" like me needed to watch out. To survive, I had to be smart. My defensive tendencies kicked in to cope with the world of arrogant teenagers whose definition of manhood was realized by intimidation. Everyone wanted to be recognized as the toughest kid – the so-called Alpha Male – in the community of confused nobodies.

CPU incorporated in its curriculum subjects like Christian Living and conducted activities like the Christian Emphasis Week. The school's values always reminded me of the light every time I wanted to go to the dark side, so to speak.

In CPU, we played a lot of pick-up basketball games during our free times. Like other contact sports, basketball is a game of aggression, albeit subtle. I'm pretty sure that was not the intention of Reverend James Naismith when he invented the sport. But the game became my refuge, and weapon at the same time. Playing it became my way of masterfully, but deviously retaliating with aggression in the name of the game.

Despite my less-than-ideal behavior, I was still privileged to play for the high school basketball varsity team during my senior year. Even now, I wonder how and why I was so blessed in school. But the best thing that ever happened to me was having my first basketball shoes! I do not know where my loving mother got the money to buy them, but I knew that the next meals she served in the days after purchasing the shoes were considerably less.

Learning the Ropes

I was a typical rambunctious teen. I tried to figure out what I would do with my life. I had a lot of questions and I didn't always seek answers from the right sources. There was a point when I wanted to pattern my life after what I saw in *The Godfather*, one of the most iconic gangster movies of all time. I was young and impressionable, so I was captivated by how the mobsters handled "the business." I liked the fact that they had so much power, but I didn't like their activities. There was still enough of a good Christian in me to realize that they were engaged in criminal pursuits. I couldn't handle that. As fascinated as I was with the idea of being a mobster, I knew deep inside me I was not made for it. I knew their activities were not only illegal but selfish and excessive as well. I wanted to be in a setting where I could expend my youthful aggression for a good cause – at least my own definition of what was "good."

I was a restless soul. I joined Kappa Phi Sigma, or ΚΦΣ, and more locally known as "*KAUGYON*," a fraternity-sorority in West Visayas State University (WVSU), during my sophomore year in college. I joined for a host of reasons – primarily to satisfy my yearning to be part of a group. It was my good friend Sheridan Gotico, who is now a successful businessman, who recruited me. Sheridan convinced me to join them after being introduced to the group's philosophy and ideals. But before formalizing my membership, I brought along my best friend Voltaire Jacinto, who is now a professor in our university, to join me. Voltaire and I officially received our membership following the group's traditional rites of passage sometime in July 1988.

The three of us – Sheridan, Voltaire, and I – have remained great friends to this day. Everyone who has joined fraternities and sororities knows what I am talking about. The organization taught me about academic excellence, brotherhood, camaraderie, and responsibility. We did a lot of things for the good of the university. Then again, we also did a lot of things that are not worthy of being mentioned at all. To its credit, *KAUGYON* produced doctors, lawyers, teachers, military officers, police officers, teachers, and businessmen. No doubt, my affiliation with the group contributed to who I am and where I am today.

Failing is Learning

In 1988, while busy with my fraternity duties and other activities outside of school, I also learned about the PMA. I had seen some cadets on vacation. They looked very tough and confident. I was told that PMA cadets were like government scholars who got paid while they were studying in the academy. I did more research about being a cadet. I learned that upon graduation they would be serving the Army, Air Force, and Navy of the Armed Forces of the Philippines. I also learned that "*PMAyers*," as they are called, went on to be combat heroes. After retirement, they would have opportunities to occupy major government positions.

I was trying to find my purpose in life and I was convinced that being admitted into the PMA was the right path for me. That thought gave a big boost to my pride and my ego. I saw it as an opportunity to be a tough guy for a good cause. I would have a noble purpose. I thought that if I got killed in the line of duty, I'd get a flag draped over my casket. My family, especially my beloved parents, would be proud of me. I thought that was worth dying for. As they say, I found my life's goal!

As I studied the profile of *PMAyers*, I noted that most of them were valedictorians or salutatorians of their high school classes. Most of them excelled in mathematics and technical subjects. I met some alumni and they oozed with confidence. The way they carried themselves seemed like a natural thing. I liked the toughness, but I didn't like the overconfidence. Much more so, I didn't like the veiled arrogance of some.

The PMA curriculum was patterned after that of the United States Military Academy (USMA) at West Point, New York. I realized I had challenges – serious ones. I was not even among the top of my class. Nor was I good in mathematics and technical subjects. Nevertheless, I decided to give it a shot.

I took the PMA Entrance Examination (PMAEE) in 1988. By then, I was already in my sophomore year at West Visayas State University (WVSU). I was working towards a Bachelor of Science degree in Social Sciences. I was planning to be a lawyer. I was the team captain of our debate team. I always felt that I didn't deserve to hold that particular position but I accepted it anyway.

With my ardent desire to be a PMA cadet one day, I took the PMA Entrance Examination (PMAEE). I was one of the 8,000 PMA examinees and became one of the 699 who passed the PMAEE. Of the 699, only 250 would eventually be admitted to join the PMA Class of 1993. I did not make it after a series of physical, medical, and neuro-psychiatric tests conducted at the AFP Medical Center in Quezon City. I accepted the outcome and told myself, *"The PMA was not for me."* I shrugged it off and thought it was time to change my "life's goal." It was time to move on.

Second Time's the Charm

I got so busy with basketball that I totally forgot about PMA. My tuition was free throughout my university days because I played for WVSU. This, despite the fact that the school is an academically-focused university and was not known for offering scholarships to top athletes.

Our basketball team was not really good, but I guess the university wanted to take a chance on us. We couldn't compete with big universities in our city but we were competitive against other state colleges and universities. We even won the Western Visayas Championship for State Colleges and Universities Athletic Association (SCUAA) and competed in the national SCUAA in March 1989. It was good enough for me. After all, my priority was to play competitive basketball at any level that I could.

I also played for my town's basketball team. We competed against the teams of different towns in our district and several other basketball tournaments. We won the Lopez Cup, a locally-known basketball tournament in the 2nd Legislative District of Iloilo province in May of 1989. I relished those days as I felt like I was in my own "happy little world" while playing basketball every chance I got. The basketball court became my comfort zone. It was my home. I felt free the moment I stepped onto the court. The PMA was no longer in my mind.

Then, one rainy day in June 1990, there was a knock on our door. It was my former basketball coach Nestor Alcudia, a retired Ensign of the Philippine Navy.

My former coach was the brother of Major General Quintin Alcudia, a member of PMA Class of 1962. MGen Alcudia had two sons – one was a member of PMA "*Tanglaw-Diwa*" Class of 1992, and the other of PMA "*Maalab*" Class of 1993. Both were PMA cadets at that time. Coach Nestor patiently talked me into taking the PMAEE again. He even brought me an application form for the PMAEE.

Eventually, Coach Nestor convinced me that I had the potential to join the military academy, and later the Armed Forces. I explained to him, however, that I already tried to get into the PMA in 1988. I reasoned that I already accepted the fact that the PMA was not for me. Yet, he insisted that I should give it another try.

After further encouragement from him, I agreed to try again. This time, I was one of the 1,000 who passed the examination out of the 10,0000 examinees. Finally, I made it into the portals of PMA in Baguio City on April 1, 1991 after passing the entire physical and medical process conducted on us at the AFP Medical Center in Quezon City. I realized later I made it to the academy not because I was smart but because God had His own plans for me. Truly, the best was yet to come.

The Academy

The PMA, or simply the "Academy" – as we alumni call her – has a long history of shaping the people who would serve as guardians of the country. The PMA asserts, "A PMA graduate is a values-centered leader who possesses the character, the broad and basic military skills, and the education essential to the successful pursuit of a progressive military career in selfless service to the AFP and the nation." The Academy also emphasizes that "a PMA graduate is a motivated leader who has imbibed the PMA core values, serves as a role model, acts as a mentor, and exhibits both moral soundness and ethical responsibility in the performance of expected roles."

The PMA formally traces its roots back to 1905, when it was an officers' school for the Philippine Constabulary in Intramuros, Manila. Then, in 1935, it was formally created via Commonwealth Act No. 1, which was known as the National Defense Act.

By 1908, the PMA was relocated to Baguio City. Its first location was at Constabulary Hill (later renamed Camp Henry T. Allen, after the first chief of the PCA). By 1938, it moved to Teacher's Camp until World War II broke out in 1941.

After the war, PMA operations resumed and the campus returned to Camp Henry T. Allen. Then, in 1950, it moved to its current home in Fort Gregorio del Pilar in Loakan, Baguio City.

All throughout the milestones and upheavals that it has faced, the PMA has stood strong. It has also evolved with the times. Yet, it is undoubtedly its timeless tradition of upholding honor and integrity that has sustained its legacy.

•••••

My Family. (Standing L-R) My late brother Roy, Linnea, Helen, and Ednathan. (Seated L-R) Rey, Vinia, my late father Fabian, Jessie, my mother Virginia, and myself. (ca. 1972)

CPU-DHS Basketball Varsity Team. (Top Row L-R) Myself, Victor Umahag, and David Braña. (Middle Row L-R) Nel Hernando, Ferdinand Manuel Jover, Ronaldo Golez, and Fritz Dela Cruz. (Bottom Row L-R) Dalton Doromal, Randolph Francisco, Edmund Abapo, Royce Reyes, Coach Hernando Agriam, Melvin Acanto, Ian Feliciano and Regan John Monton.

Lopez Cup. 2nd Legislative District Basketball Tournament Champion. (Standing L-R) Benmar Altubar, Noel Saclote, myself, James Remyr Lobaton, Eduardo Pineda, Zandro Rodriguez, Larry Alderete, Ronald Ambut, Jemuel Amba, and Stephen Altubar. (Kneeling L-R) Cyrus Alejo, Samson Alinsasaguin, and Ashley Allado (ca. 1989)

Kappa Phi Sigma (Kaugyon) Frasority, West Visayas State University. (Standing L-R) Armstrong Tingson, Bien Paul Obordo, Jorge Borja and myself. (Sitting L-R) Victor Deala, Nelia Lingaya, Benjie Bauson, Rex Yumen, Sheridan Gotico, Jessica Castro, Robinson Raymundo, Joylin Pilla, and Eden Portillo (ca. 1988).

The Plebe

The Picnic. To my left was my squad mate Cdt Nilo Arribas

Incorporation Day. The day that marked the incorporation of the plebes to the Cadet Corps Armed Forces of the Philippines. (May 1991)

(L-R) Cdt Jay Anibigno, Cdt Joey Escanillas ('93), myself and Cdt Nilo Arribas

The Yearling

(L-R) Cdt Levi Palomo ('93), myself, Cdt Aristotle Fuertes ('94), Cdt Sherwin Respeto ('96), Neil Cristal ('94), Cdt Benjamin Go ('96), Cdt Leo Dimoc ('96), Cdt Victor Gavino ('95)

My Yearling Squadmates. (L-R) Cdt Victor Gavino, Cdt Edwin Divina, Cdt Ronald Ruiz ('93), my former squad leader during my plebe year, myself, and Cdt Jones Otida.

Hawk Hunters in athletic uniform. (ca. 1993)

The Cow

Cdt Normandy Biagtas and I receiving the plebes of PMA Class of 1997 (April 1, 1993)

(L-R) Cdt Jay Anibigno, Cdt Joe Macapili, Cdt Fermin Mabulo, Cdt Jones Otida, and myself. (ca. 1993)

My yearling squadmates. Cdt Benjamin Go, myself, Cdt Leo Dimoc, and Cdt Sherwin Respeto. (ca. 1993)

Parade and Review. (L-R) Cdt Fermin Mabulo, myself, and Cdt Sandy David.

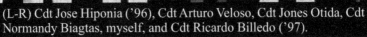

(L-R) Cdt Jose Hiponia ('96), Cdt Arturo Veloso, Cdt Jones Otida, Cdt Normandy Biagtas, myself, and Cdt Ricardo Billedo ('97).

Ring Hop. (L-R) My late father Fabian, my Kaydet Girl Ena, myself, and my mother Virginia

Receiving my Diploma. (L-R) MGen Rodolfo S. Estrellado, PMA Superintendent, and Philippine President Fidel Valdez Ramos

The Firstie

March 4, 1995 - Graduation of PMA *"Marilag"* Class of 1995 with President Fidel Valdez Ramos as the Guest of Honor and Speaker.

CHAPTER 3

PMA *"MARILAG"* CLASS OF 1995

"The Lord will fulfill his purpose for me;
your steadfast love, O LORD, endures forever.
Do not forsake the work of your hands."

— Psalm 138:8 (ESV)

My four years at the PMA were filled with challenges. Each and every PMA cadet has a very interesting story to tell. All these stories are fascinating. Nothing compares to the experience of being at the academy.

I often heard from those who were ahead of us: "There are two ways to get out of this institution. One, is to get dismissed for whatever reason, and two, is to graduate." I soon found out that getting out the right way was not going to be easy.

There were a lot of cadets who seemed to have everything. They had the intelligence, good looks, and physical abilities. I was not one of them. Yet, I was baffled when some of those cadets were not able to graduate.

There were cadets who were very intelligent, but got dismissed for violations of the anti-hazing policy. They had resorted to maltreatment as a method of discipline. Strange form of discipline, but some say that the "rigorous mental and physical calisthenics" are just apt training for someone being readied to tread the worst of conditions in the future. Simply put, hazing is one form of 'rigorous calisthenics' designed to toughen up the cadets who will one day meet someone else tougher than them.

There were cadets who were athletically gifted, but they got dismissed because of academic deficiencies.

There were those who had both the intelligence and athletic gifts, but lacked the intestinal fortitude to endure and persevere.

Then, there were some who were expelled from the academy for violating the Honor Code which states, *"We the cadets do not lie, cheat or steal nor tolerate those who do."* Strict adherence to the Honor Code is a must, and violation of it carries outright dismissal from the Academy.

My Beloved Class

I belong to the very socially-diverse and ideologically-interesting PMA *"Marilag"* Class of 1995.

Out of 10,000 examinees, 1,000 passed the Entrance Examination. I myself couldn't believe that I made it the second time – no doubt a divine intervention.

After the physical, medical, and neuro-psychiatric tests, around 250 of us were appointed as fourth class cadets by Corazon Cojuangco-Aquino, the then President of the Republic of the Philippines. Finally, I said to myself, *"Yes, I will now be able to step foot on the hallowed ground of Borromeo Field."* But little did I know that on that hallowed ground, my thousands of agonizing hours would officially commence. Call it the start of a funny-fulfilling journey that I would gladly take for the next several years of my life.

The Borromeo Field is one of PMA's most sacred grounds. To my knowledge, no one has dared break its unwritten rule of *"never cross it from end to end in a whim"*, unless during officially sanctioned activities or for exigent circumstances. Borromeo

Field is used for many cadet activities, mainly to mark special occasions in a cadet's life. In the words of Alfred McCoy (1999), "From Incorporation Day where they are formally recognized as PMA plebes; to Recognition Day where they receive their laurels for being Third Class officers; and to their much-awaited Graduation Day which makes them official members of the Armed Forces of the Philippines, the Borromeo Field is a silent witness to many memorable events; it also hosts the worst ones: from summer camp where qualified applicants undergo the much-dreaded "Beast Barracks"

Our class name *"Marilag"* means *"highest form of excellence"*. Whether we lived up to the ideals we were taught and revered, only history can determine. Time will unravel who we are, what have we become, and what we did in our lifetime – whether our actions are considered good or otherwise. After all, perspective is a powerful argument.

Ours, PMA Class '95, is the first class with a tri-service curriculum. In our third year, we were separated according to the branch of service where we would go. The Air Force cadets took the Bachelor of Science in Aeronautical Science; the Navy cadets took Bachelor of Science in Naval Systems Engineering; and the Army cadets took Bachelor of Science in Management.

Plebehood

During my first year, or "plebe year", at the PMA, I was assigned to the Hawk Company – the best company, according to its members, in the Cadet Corps Armed Forces of the Philippines (CCAFP). There were eight companies all in all. Aside from Hawk, there were Alpha, Bravo, Charlie, Delta, Echo, Foxtrot, and Golf companies.

Plebe year was the toughest, as I had to make the transition from the life of a civilian to the regimented life of someone in the military. In the first two months at the PMA, we, plebes, underwent "The Beast Barracks." As a part of it, we had to learn the Plebe Knowledges. These were cadet doctrines and affirmations that had to be memorized ad infinitum – no more, no less. There were a lot, but these are a few of them: *How Long is Eternity?, Don't Quit, and Are you Resigning?*

We were told that memorizing the Plebe Knowledges would enhance our memorizing skills and, as such, prepare us for our academics. I didn't appreciate our training back then. I could barely survive the day. Here's a sample of a Plebe Knowledge that describes the way I felt during this time.

"How Long Is Eternity?"

"Sir, if it takes a bird from outer space traveling at the speed of a turtle that is taking his time and picks a grain of sand from the earth and brings it back to the place where he came from and deposits it there and does the process once in every million years, and after picking all the minute grains of sand on earth and depositing them on the bank of the galaxies of heaven, he brings them back to their places, eternity shall have just begun. I hope that the lazy and dumb bird will travel forth and my chinning and double-timing be made shorter than the beginning of eternity, Sir!"

Indeed, my first year seemed like an eternity. We were not allowed to go home until after a year so it was rough for all of us plebes. Everything seemed to be a blur for me back then. Quitting cadetship was the easiest way out of the academy for me but again, quitting was the last thing on my mind. After all, to never quit was drilled into my system via one of the timeless Plebe Knowledges,

"Don't Quit"

When things go wrong as they sometimes will,
When the road you're trudging seems all uphill,
When the funds are low and the debts are high,

And you want to smile but you have to sigh.
When care is pressing you down a bit,
Rest if you must, but don't you quit.

Life is queer with its twists and turns,
As everyone of us sometimes learns,
And many a failure turns about.
When he might have won had he stuck it out;
Don't give up though the pace seems slow –
You may succeed with another blow.

Often the goal is nearer than.
It seems to a faint and faltering man.
Often the struggler has given up
When he might have won the victor's cup,
And he learned too late when the light came down,
How close he was to the golden crown.

Success is failure turned inside out.
The silver tint of the clouds of doubt,
And you never can tell how close you are.
It may be near when it seems far;
So stick to the fight when you're hardest hit,
It's when things seem worst that you must not quit.

There were times when our upperclassmen, particularly the senior cadets of Hawk company, would mentally intimidate us by saying that "H" stands for hazing. Under calculated pressure, some would unfortunately cave in. And after bombarding us with tons of mind-boggling questions enough to make us doubt our ability to survive the rigors of cadetship, the quintessential question would finally be dropped on us, *"Are you resigning?"*, to which we would answer in unison at the top of our lungs,

"Sir, I came from the land of the Kings, where everyone can do what he wishes. I hike the plains of Luzon and hurdled the mountains of Baguio just to reach my precious destination, the Philippine Military Academy.

Now, I am here as a plebe, a ducrot to the third classmen, a chicken to the second classmen and a good neighbor to the first classmen. Now, are you resigning? No sir, over the dead and rotten body of Fourth Classman Almonares, Sir!"

Heaven on Earth

In the Academy, one of the things I loved most was attending church, which I took advantage of sometimes. Cadets were allowed to practice their religious beliefs and required to attend their respective religious activities every weekend, or on designated worship days. The majority of my Christian upperclassmen were very kind, considerate and gracious – very typical qualities of a believer which can sometimes be taken advantage of depending on the kind of environment.

As a rotting plebe, to be inside the church felt like heaven compared to the hellish barracks where all one heard were the shouts and curses of upperclassmen and voices of confused fourthclassmen. Yes, being inside-barracks was mind-numbing. A plebe, to survive, needed not to think of other things. A plebe only needed to think of ways and ideas that would allow him/her to survive the daily ordeal in a topsy-turvy world that was deliberately designed for him/her and his/her fellow plebes.

Inside the church, the sound of the musical organ and singing of hymns during Sundays brought a lot of us to tears. I guess it was mixed emotions of worship and serious homesickness. The civilians who worshipped with us were so kind and supportive. They gave us a lot of comfort, and on special occasions, good food too! Hands down, the last one was the best part.

Cadets like myself attending Christian services were relaxed during meals and went back to the barracks late. However, the Holy Mass – a one-hour spiritual celebration of Catholics in the Philippines, usually finished early. Hence, as soon as my esteemed Catholic classmates got back to the barracks, a "*mase-*

mase" or mass exercise was done in unison until the next meal commenced. On the other hand, Christian services finished late, thus, giving us a little bit more free time before we joined the other plebes. Every little respite was a priceless treasure – such was my mindset at that time! It might be a fleshly advantage but I truly valued the spiritual opportunity to worship God amid the stringent implementation of regimented activities.

But if there was one thing that I cherished most in my plebe year, which I continue to cherish now, it was playing basketball during weekends with my two very competitive upperclassmen – Cadet Westrimundo Domantay Obinque and Cadet Rommel Gabuat Reyes. Both graduated as distinguished members of PMA "*Tanglaw-Diwa*" Class of 1992. In basketball as in cadet life, they both imparted a lot of wisdom to me on how to survive the PMA and graduate. They truly created a huge impact on my life.

2Lt Obinque would later join the Philippine National Police (PNP); while 2Lt Reyes was killed-in-action (KIA) while bravely leading his platoon of Philippine Marines during a combat operation in the island of Sulu, Mindanao.

Precious Redemptions

As Plebes, we were subjected to endless "*mase-mase*" or any activity that would preoccupy our minds to prevent the thought of quitting, or going AWOL by escaping the premises of PMA. Our upperclassmen or senior cadets were hardcore adherents to the timeless adage, "An idle mind is the devil's playground." Hence, the philosophy for our perpetual physical agony – *mase-mase* all the way!

So, to keep the "devil" away from our consciousness, we performed different physical exercises en masse and in unison – conducted by the Second Classmen and Third Classmen – each weekend. Every session was an activity that produced buckets of sweat, and sometimes tears. But often in the midst of it all, the imposing and thundering voices of my two First Classmen basketball players would interrupt the activity.

"Fourth Classman Almonares! Pull out!"

"Ahh! Thank God for basketball!" I said to myself, as I rejoiced deep down with my fortune. *"I was liberated again from physical misery."* In the Academy, any useful talent – be it in sports, arts or other fields – could give you much-needed respite from the grueling training. Every moment of free-and-easy time is a windfall of fortune to any cadet, particularly to a fourthclassman.

To me, hearing the familiar voices of my two upperclassmen were like those of "angels beckoning me and freeing me up from my misery." Being called out from the formation was heaven-on-earth at that time. It meant that I was exempted (again) from hardship and was being cordially invited instead to enjoy the sport I love most – basketball. There is a temporal heaven indeed, I thought.

However, after the basketball game and right outside the court, it was all back to reality in an instant. Everything seemed to be hazy-crazy. All plebes must always be on the double. Time is always of the essence in the military. We were trained to always be ready to think and decide accordingly on our feet – for in extreme circumstances, such as in battle, there is no luxury of time. In the military academy, events and actions were designed to be fast-paced. Hence, every time we were challenged by senior cadets, particularly the Firstclassmen, with the question, *"Why on the double?"* our ready reply was always,

> "Sir, the answer is very simple. The forces coming from the itinerate glances of the Immaculates are so powerful that the circulation of the corpuscles of the plebes upon which the stare is applied is integrated. This results in the gyrostatic effect on the paradoxical interior of the legs, thus, double-timing ensues. This develops

an invulnerable machine in the body of the degraded mammal due to the action of the rectilinear eyes, Sir."

And, from time to time, some upperclassmen – to add more spice to our cadet life – would also ask us *"How is life?"* We were ready with our answer.

"Sir, life is as monotonous as the curvilinear concubitant wave of the peristaltic motion of a dilated cell. It is as tense as the state existing among the molecules of a highly compressed gas. As barren as the deserts of Africa where plants never grow. As gloomy as the thoughts of a thousand eunuchs on the death of Cleopatra. As hopeless as the crew of Christopher Columbus panic-stricken in the sea of darkness. As discouraging as the graceful shape of the adiabatic curve. As smooth as the sine curve, endless as the parabola, stubborn as the catenary, and meaningless as an imaginary function. Its memory brings an extraordinary sensation which tickles the convolutions of the brain and the cells of the spinal cord. In plain and simple language, life is a conglomeration of things too serious for a fool to appreciate, Sir!"

But at the end of every day, a plebe would realize that everything he had confidently absorbed was hazy and that he had still a lot to learn after being asked and having answered the question *"Do you understand?"*

"Sir, my cranium consisting of Vermont marble, volcanic lava and African ivory, covered with a thick layer of case-hardened steel, forms an impenetrable barrier to all that seeks to impress itself upon the ashen tissues of my brain. Hence, the effulgent and ostentatiously effervescent phrases just now directed and reiterated for my comprehension have failed to penetrate the coniferous forest of my atrocious intelligence. In other words, I am very dumb and I do not understand, Sir!"

To be a plebe is interesting. One must be philosophical, and humble, for a host of reasons – but oftentimes to survive the rigors of military training.

•••

Plebes are not supposed to play sports like basketball. They are sports intended for the upperclassmen to enjoy, especially in Hawk Company. But if it's the desire of the Immaculate, it will surely come to pass. Plebes are supposed to play combative sports. It may be a simple thing for others, but to me those basketball weekends were always a form of redemption.

At some point, I failed Algebra and almost got dismissed. Fortunately, I was one of those who were given a second chance – a very clear manifestation of God's grace through the fair academic system. It never crossed my mind to resign or quit cadetship. *"Hindi bale matanggal sa PMA dahil sa bagsak sa academics, huwag lang ako voluntary mag-resign o mag-quit."* [It doesn't matter if I get dismissed from PMA because of academic failure, but I'll never leave PMA because I voluntarily resigned or had quit]. This became my personal battle cry. It may be funny, but that 'never-say-die' attitude worked well for me even after I graduated from PMA.

So, how's Cadet Fourthclassman Almonares in his plebehood year?

"Sir, Cadet Almonares, he is the symbol of all that is bold and handsome, in the grand posture of a dashing gentleman, and the warm and tender lips of a great lover in the mystic smile of a victorious soldier in the masculine build of an Olympian God and a courage of a thousand warriors. He walks with the strength of a lion and with the gentleness of the morning wind. His personality smacks at the solid rocks that kick the rushing waves of the shore. His eyes are as brown as roasty chestnuts clear and tantalizing glows with the rays of the settling sun.

In short and simple language, Cadet Almonares is very handsome, Sir!

Yes, I was very much alive and kicking after a year in PMA. I survived!

Yearling

In my second year, I did well in my social sciences subjects, but had a hard time with technical subjects. I did well in Trigonometry but failed in Integral Calculus. Again, by God's amazing grace, I passed it the second time around. The "back subject" system was implemented in our time so the government could save money. It meant that cadets were given a chance to take the failed subject again the next semester instead of making them join the next class the following year. It worked well for me.

Compared to my plebe year, where every moment seemed to be a blur in a world full of remarkable traditions and meaningful philosophy, my yearling year – or second year as a cadet – was far kinder. I had already adjusted to the regimented life in the academy. But if my upperclassmen would ask me about how I was doing as a yearling cadet that time, I had my prescribed reply.

"Sir, from the simple handshake of recognition to the rotting days of academics, the yearling is still at a loss under the scrutinizing eyes of the firstclassmen, the witty jokes of the secondclassmen, and the extreme laxities of the fourthclassmen. The yearling, given only a few months of rapid growth will develop into a young cow, Sir!"

At any rate, I passed my 2nd year in one piece with my sanity intact. No complaints.

Cow Year

In my third year or cow year, Army cadets took management subjects in preparation for a career in the Philippine Army. I didn't have many technical subjects, which proved to be a blessing as I was not that good at it. Without my Waterloo subjects, I did well, and even managed to improve my class standing. But that was not really my concern. I was just trying my best to survive academics and leave the academy as a graduate.

The subjects I really excelled in during my third year as a cadet were Ethics and Philosophy. Never in my mind did I think that those subjects and long hours of cerebral discussions were preparing my person for what I will become someday. But now I know and understand it well.

And basketball? We earned a spot for the National Intercollegiate Basketball Tournament after we won as 1st Runner Up in the highly-competetive Baguio Colleges and Universities Athletic Association (BCUAA) in 1993. We played against future Philippine basketball professionals like Kenneth Duremdes and EJ Feihl. The PMA contingent was short on height and size but full of heart and determination.

Immaculate Year

Perhaps, my last year in the PMA could be summed up by asking, *"How's the Firstie?"*

> "Sir, the Firstie? He is wondering about the intricate remedies of law, the solution of the debt and credit in economics, bewildered by the unorthodox strategies of tactics and military history, failing from his structure and design, blown up by the ultramodern weapon of Ordnance, and confused by the government set-up of Political Science. In short and simple language, the Firstie say, "I'm leaving in a jet plane, Sir".

My fourth and final year in PMA was not really challenging academically compared to prior years. Those who were at the top of our class did their best to improve their respective standings in the class. But for a mediocre like myself, I tried to make the most of my remaining days as a cadet and prayed I would survive PMA.

Firstclassmen are called "Immaculates". I do not fully agree with the name because that word is defined as *"having no stain or having no flaw or error."* In the strictest sense, the only person I know having no flaw or stain is Jesus!

Anyway, the word "Immaculates" was used in the context that whatever was commanded, the underclassmen would follow and take as absolute. Great power was given to us coupled with great responsibility. The idea was for us to practice leading our men on the battlefield. Decisions, right or wrong, must be made in combat situations where there are many life and death situations. In such chaotic and pressured scenarios, long debates and discussions have no place.

Looking back, and using the lens of a true Christian, I can say we made a lot of poor choices and decisions in the guise of being *"Immaculates.* The adage, "Absolute power corrupts absolutely" is true. Power should have restraints, checks and balances.

Moral and legal regulations put up barriers to the potential of possible excesses in any form of governance – be it in leadership or followership. Many cadets in their final year were dismissed because of lack of restraint and good judgement. Honestly, I was one of those. But by God's divine providence, He allowed me to survive because He had a portion for me to perform in the years to come. While allowing some of cadets with brilliant minds to be dismissed, gifting a mediocre person like me with success still baffles me to this day. The best way I can describe this is to refer to what the Apostle Paul said to believers in *Romans 9:15 (NLT),*

"For God said to Moses, 'I will show mercy to anyone I choose, and I will show compassion to anyone I choose'."

Diverse, Unique, and Interesting

Each one in our class was unique, but we all aimed to be the best – be it in academics, sports, personal pursuits, or even in just doing simple things. All PMA classes traditionally claim that theirs is the best. For good measure, some declare it jokingly but others do so with perpetual conviction and utmost confidence. Unfortunately, some upperclassmen were deeply, or otherwise, inclined to think that they were smarter than their underclassmen just because they graduated ahead of them. I found it funny, but I guess that's part of human nature and depravity. On a positive note, there are still a lot of level-headed upperclassmen who know when and where to say their piece without disturbing the peace.

However, there were disturbing instances in Philippine politics when some PMA graduates, especially those who are now in politics, engaged in ungentlemanly clashes as they defended their respective political stances. Each one of them, of course, believed he was right and that his cause was the only one that is just and sound. Each had to do what he needed to do according to his own personal perspective and political convictions.

That has been the problem of man since the beginning of time,

---

[2] The Oakwood Mutiny, or sometimes referred to as the "Oakwood Incident", happened on July 27, 2003 when hundreds of AFP junior officers and their colleagues tookover the Oakwood Premier Ayala Center in Makati City. The event was to openly show to the Filipino people the alleged massive corruption in the government, particularly in the administration of then President Gloria Macapagal-Arroyo. The group was later labeled "*Magdalo*" by the media, in reference to the insignia – the eight-rayed sun version of the Philippine flag used by the "*Magdalo*" faction of the Philippine Revolution at the turn of the 19th Century – that the former adopted during the incident.

and I humbly understand that each has a position when it comes to the seemingly unfathomable political spectrum. It is complicated and it boggles my mind. I don't fully understand it, I must admit.

In Biblical times, even the apostles James and John, sons of Zebedee, in *Mark 10:37 (ESV)* asked this from Jesus:

"Grant us to sit, one at your right and one at your left, in your glory."

The other apostles, upon hearing this, were not happy. *Mark 10:41 (ESV)* says,

"And when the ten heard about it, they began to be indignant at James and John." The disciples resented James and John for their attempt to gain an advantage over the others in pursuing the honor they all wanted."

Man has the strong tendency to pursue his own glory, even to the point of death, whether it is his enemy's or his own. Human depravity is exhibited in pride, the mother of all sins.

"Pride goes before destruction, and a haughty spirit before a fall." *Proverbs 16:18 (ESV)*

This is very evident in our society. Just take a look at our own respective social circles. But here's the truth: I was this person, too. I suffered the consequences of my actions. This is true for me and for anyone else. No man can change another man. Only Jesus Christ, "the author and finisher of our faith", can do that *(Hebrews 12:2)*.

The *Marilags*

Here are some of my classmates who made an impact in Philippine society in one way or the other. The impact may vary depending on what side of the social or political fence one is on. But let me make things clear first, I'm not into electoral politics.

I'm just grateful and blessed to have known these people, some more closely than others, at some point in my life. They were my classmates after all. I never thought that out of the millions of young Filipinos of my age at that time they would become my PMA classmates.

Indeed, life is full of surprises just as Forrest Gump in his namesake movie (1994) once said, *"Life is like a box of chocolates, you never know what you're going to get."* Among my classmates who are now public personalities, or have been thrust into the public arena, are:

Cpt Gerardo *"Geri"* Gambala, our class valedictorian whom we fondly call *"Kaspog"*, short for *"Kasi Pogi"*. He was a seasoned Scout Ranger officer – being a member of SR Class 140-00 – assigned for many years in the ZamBaSulTa (Zamboanga-Basilan-Sulu-Tawi-tawi) area. He was one of the leaders of the Oakwood Mutiny . Imprisoned for five years, Geri was spiritually rescued inside the prison and is now an active evangelist advancing the gospel of Jesus Christ.

Senator Antonio *"Sonny"* Trillanes IV, a former Lieutenant Senior Grade (LTSG) of the Philippine Navy, was another leader of the Oakwood Mutiny who eventually won a Senate seat while in prison. He was among the top graduates in our PMA class wherein he also received the Mathematics Plaque, Physical Science Plaque, and the Tambuli Award for electrical/electronics engineering. *Sonny* is about to complete on June 30, 2019 his 12-year stint as Senator of the Republic of the Philippines.

Representative Gary Alejano, was a former Captain of the Philippine Marines and was also one of the leaders of the Oakwood Mutiny. He later became a congressman under the Magdalo Party-list. A seasoned Philippine Marine Corps Force Recon officer, Gary had his time on the battlefield. He was wounded in action and was recommended for the Medal of Valor for exceptional and conspicuous gallantry in action during the all-out war in Mindanao in 2000.

Several of my classmates became lawyers, businessmen, politicians, officials in different government and non-government agencies, and many are still actively defending the freedom of our country. Those who remained in the military service are now Lieutenant Colonels and will eventually become top military leaders. They continue to be our soldier-heroes to this day – steadfast and dedicated to military life. I cannot write all the names of my PMA classmates and their respective accomplishments, but they are no less remarkable. Let's just say, and I believe, that writing about all of them and their splendid exploits will have to wait to be told in another book.

Most of my classmates are notable in their own right. For example, the one whom I co-wrote this book with is a notable quiet professional. Truly, I feel so blessed and grateful that I was given an opportunity to be a part of PMA Class '95. God had a specific purpose for all of us.

From our viewpoint, we do things that interest us personally, especially when they are aligned with our values. We did what we need to do to accomplish the task at hand. But in God's economy, He will accomplish His purposes no matter what. He is sovereign.

As for me, I am who I am right now because of God's grace and mercy through Jesus Christ our Lord and Savior. I believe that is also true of them, to all of us who believe. Amazing grace indeed.

"Many are the plans in the mind of a man, but it is the purpose of the Lord that will stand." *Proverbs 19:21 (ESV)*

New Enemies

As it turned out, the early 1990s ushered in a new batch of terrorists that the nation's armed forces would eventually face.

In 1991, the Abu Sayyaf Group (ASG) was founded by Abdurajak Abubakar Janjalani. The ASG was tagged as a breakaway group from the Moro National Liberation Front (MNLF). The Abu Sayyaf objected to the fact that the MNLF had engaged in peace talks with the government, which led to the establishment of the Autonomous Region in Muslim Mindanao (ARMM). The ASG did not want to pursue autonomy. They wanted to establish an independent Islamic state.

Janjalani was a former Filipino Islamic scholar who studied Islamic theology and Arabic in Libya, Syria, and Saudi Arabia in the 1980s. He went on to join the war against the Soviets in Afghanistan. It was during this time that the ASG founder allegedly met Osama Bin Laden.

Indeed, the ASG was initially funded by Bin Laden's brother-in-law Mohammed Jamal Khalifa. He had come to to the Philippines in the late 1980s to serve as the head of the Philippine branch of the International Islamic Relief Organization (IIRO). The IIRO was presented as a charity organization.

In the paper "Balik-Terrorism: The Return of the Abu Sayyaf" – written by Zachary Abuza and submitted to the Strategic Studies Institute (SSI) of the U.S. Army War College – an ASG defector said that the IIRO was just a front. The defector pointed out: "Only 10 to 30 percent of the foreign funding goes to the legitimate relief and livelihood projects and the rest goes to terrorist operations." Through IIRO, Al-Qaeda provided the ASG with funding and training when it was initially set up.

Al-Qaeda is the militant Sunni Islamist multinational organization that was founded in 1988 by Bin Laden, Palestinian Sunni Islamic scholar Abdullah Yusuf Azzam, and several other Arab volunteers in the war against the Soviets in Afghanistan. By 1995, the ASG became active in bombings and attacks. That year, the *Marilag* class graduated from the PMA on March 4. The following month, the ASG attacked the town of Ipil – which is located in the province of Zamboanga Sibugay in Mindanao.

•••••

PHILIPPINE MILITARY

(Top Row L-R) Cdt Franklin Fabic, Cdt Randy Buena, Cdt Alvin Hate, Cdt Arturo Veloso. (Middle Row L-R) Cdt Sandy David, Cdt Jones Otida, Cdt Mark Joseph Delos Santos. (Bottom Row L-R) Myself, and Cdt Ronauld Tabora. (ca. 1992)

(L-R) Cdt Dante Langkit, Cdt Ian Ferrer and myself. (May 1993)

(L-R) Myself, Cdt Jovito Palo, Cdt Carlo Ferrer, Cdt Russell Mascardo and the late Ricky Chua.

Weapons Training (May 1993)

Marilag Army Group (ca. 1994)

The *"Marilags"*... then and now.

Meeting my Retired Air Force Classmate. Frolics with Froi Paras, whom I have not met for almost 20 years, during the Jurado Cup 2015 in Illinois, USA - a gathering of PMA graduates and associates all around the globe.

Meeting the Senator after 23 years. (L-R) Myself, Sen. Antonio *"Sonny"* Trillanes IV and Eric Agudelo (February 2018)

Reunion of the Army, Navy and Air Force. (L-R) Eric Agudelo of the Philippine Navy, who is my good neighbor in Illinois, myself of the Philippine Army and James Acosta of the Philippine Air Force, who visited us on his way to Minnesota. (March 2018)

Meeting the Congressman after 23 years. (L-R) Myself, Representative Gary Alejano, and Eric Agudelo. (November 2018)

CHAPTER 4

SCOUT RANGER GROUP '95

"I know that you can do all things,
and that no purpose of yours can be thwarted."

— *Job 42:2 (ESV)*

I graduated from PMA on March 4, 1995. Former President Fidel Valdez Ramos was the guest of honor and speaker during our graduation. He commissioned 214 of us on that day as Second Lieutenants in the Army and Air Force, and Ensigns in the Navy of the AFP.

Looking back, I get emotional thinking about God's grace and mercy. *Grace* is God giving us what we do not deserve. *Mercy* is God withholding what we deserve. I felt that I did not deserve to graduate, but I did and that was amazing grace! I could probably have been dismissed from cadetship as punishment for some of my unthinking excesses and omissions. But I was spared and that was overwhelming mercy. God touched the hearts of people involved in our training who must have seen potential in me, so they gave this wretched person a chance. Despite God constantly calling for my attention, I hardened my heart. Even after so many chances, I continued to be a captain of my own soul – one who was full of himself.

Eager to be Elite

I had my short vacation at home after my graduation from PMA, and afterwards I reported to Headquarters Philippine Army. Other newly-commissioned Army Lieutenants in my class reported back with me. The Army leadership decided to send us first to undergo officers' basic specialization courses. I chose Infantry as my specialization course. To me, being an Infantryman was the best you can be in the Army. It was the specialization that would get me closest to the battlefield. To borrow the words of the Pulitzer Prize-winning journalist Ernie Pyle, "I love the infantry because they are the underdogs. They are the mud-rain-frost-and-wind boys. They have no comforts, and they even learn to live without the necessities. And in the end, they are the guys that wars can't be won without."

After completing our officer basic course, we were asked about our preferred Army units before we were issued final orders of deployment. I proudly volunteered to be a Scout Ranger. That meant the Army would need to be convinced that I deserved to be assigned to the First Scout Ranger Regiment (FSRR) for me to eventually become an organic officer of the unit. It was a tough choice. The unit is known to really go into many serious non-stop combat operations for days, weeks and even months. To be assigned in FSRR, an elite Army unit, is a matter of pride – and I was full of it.

There were 25 officers from our PMA class who enthusiastically volunteered. Ten of us, along with a graduate from a foreign military school, were chosen. The FSRR is known as one of the best special operations unit in the world. In terms of physical fitness, I felt like I was the weakest. On hindsight, I believe I was only on the radar of the special operations recruiters because of basketball. Those veteran special operators loved basketball! I'm glad they picked me from the tough lot.

The other officers who volunteered with me and were chosen to join the First Scout Ranger Regiment of the Philippine Army were as follows:

2ⁿᵈ Lieutenant Samuel "*Sam*" Yunque (SR Class 127-97) is a good tennis and basketball player, very athletic and incredibly motivated. He is a well-decorated officer and is the former commander of the 1ˢᵗ Scout Ranger Battalion (1SRB). He is a recipient of two Distinguished Conduct Stars, five Gold Crosses, and several other combat medals in addition to the administrative medals he got from excelling in leadership. He is one of the heroes in the Battle of Marawi against the ISIS-inspired group led by the Maute brothers and other notable extremist commanders such as Isnilon Hapilon, who kidnapped the Burnham couple along with other hostages from Dos Palmas Resort in Palawan in 2001. For conspicuous gallantry in action and exemplary leadership in the successful rescue of beleaguered troops of another unit deep behind enemy lines in Marawi, Sam and his troops were aptly recognized. This particular feat was aptly chronicled in the book *NO MAN LEFT BEHIND: A Story of Valor in the Battle of Marawi*, written by Phil Fortuno, PhD.

2ⁿᵈ Lieutenant JJ "*Junjie*" Luntok (SR Class 131-97) is one of those academically gifted in our group. When we graduated, *Junjie* was among the top graduates of PMA "*Marilag*" Class of 1995. He is a trained U.S. Army Special Forces operator, and became the first commander of the Light Reaction Company – the Delta Force of the Philippines – in 2001. He currently commands the 4ᵗʰ Scout Ranger (*Masigasig*) Battalion, one of the five Scout Ranger battalions that made an indelible mark in the Battle of Marawi. Tall, athletic, and built for action – needless to say, *Junjie* is tough as nails.

2ⁿᵈ Lieutenant Milo "*Miles*" Maestrecampo (SR Class 126-96) was the valedictorian of his elementary and high school classes. He is stocky and athletic. He is a good basketball point guard and did judo for the PMA Corps Squad. He later became the commander of the 16th Scout Ranger (*Mabangis*) Company. He was imprisoned for his involvement in the Oakwood Mutiny in 2003, but was eventually pardoned. He now enjoys a quiet life as a private citizen, often volunteering and working for community development.

2nd Lieutenant Albert "*Bert*" Baloloy (SR Class 125-96) is an endurance runner. Tall, athletic and built to run, he represented the Army and FSRR in different marathon competitions. He is a trained U.S. Army Ranger. He became the commander of the 10th Scout Ranger (We Lead) Company, and led his company as a supporting effort during the rescue of the Burnham couple. He was also imprisoned for his involvement in the Oakwood Mutiny, but amazingly found faith in Jesus Christ while imprisoned. He, too, was eventually pardoned. He is now a pastor, a good soldier for the Commanding Officer of this Universe.

2nd Lieutenant William "*Bong*" Upano (SR Class 126-96) is a lean and mean kind of guy. In anything he does, he demonstrates fierce determination – whether it be in sports, combat, or fixing a broken Humvee. He is a good volleyball and basketball player. He later became the commander of the 7th Scout Ranger (*In Hoc Signo Vinces*) Company. He is still active in the service, serving as the commander of one of the Philippine Army's Forward Service Support Units in southern Philippines.

2nd Lieutenant Ian "*Tsamarts*" Martinez (SR Class 128-96) is a man of wisdom. Described by peers as cool and steady under pressure, he is very athletic and good in sports – especially basketball. We always defer to his wisdom when it comes to the intricacies of life. He is now a private citizen enjoying quiet time with his family in one of the naturally-blessed communities of the Philippines.

2nd Lieutenant Laurence "*Giant*" Somera (SR Class 125-96) is 6 feet tall, but always claims that he's just 5'11.5". He never goes to the gym despite having the body of a gym rat. He is the only one who was "sniper-trained" in the group. He later became the commander of the 18th Scout Ranger (*Makamandag*) Company. *Giant* got involved in the 2003 Oakwood Mutiny, was imprisoned, and eventually pardoned. He currently enjoys his civilian life, sporting a hermit-like beard.

2nd Lieutenant John "*Andong*" Andres (SR Class 125-96) is a natural boxer and a good basketball player as well. He is the shy type, and a laid back kind of person. *Andong* was one of the first to achieve combat recognition among us. He received several combat medals in the early part of our military careers, and later became the commander of the 14th Scout Ranger (*Mabalasik*) Company, which has its operational area on the islands of Sulu and Basilan. He was also imprisoned because of the Oakwood Mutiny, and was later pardoned. He now lives a modest and fulfilling life in a quaint local community.

2nd Lieutenant Nicolas "*Nick*" Danao (SR Class 126-96) is the "wiseguy" of the group. He is stocky and muscular, built for carrying heavy backpacks and climbing mountains. He later became the commander of the 17th Scout Ranger (*Mabagsik*) Company who made indelible marks in combat operations in the hinterlands of Luzon and Mindanao. Nick happily lives now with his family in the beautiful country of Australia. He is saved by grace and is a strong believer in Jesus Christ. He is now humbly teaching Sunday School classes to prepare Christian soldiers in their spiritual battles.

2nd Lieutenant Phil "*Fortune*" Fortuno (SR Class 131-97) is a graduate of the Singapore Armed Forces Officer Cadet School. *Fortune*, a former seminarian, has the looks of the "boy next door" and often appears harmless. His scholarly persona, however, hides his fiery Scout Ranger heart and remarkable military history. After his overseas stint, he reported to FSRR and was warmly welcomed as our esteemed *"mistah"*, a distinct endearment for a classmate in the military academy. He later became the commander of the 2nd Scout Ranger (*Venceremos*) Company. At present, *Fortune* keeps himself busy in farmworks while contemplating the wonders of life in his tranquil coffee moments.

Looking back, I can fairly say that our Scout Ranger Group '95 was an interesting bunch of young idealists who dared to take on the challenge as best as we could at that time. Figuratively, we felt we were ready to conquer the world, even with our bare hands. But in reality, we had so much to learn in the intricacies of soldiery.

Echo-Echo

All of us volunteer-officers went through a rigorous six-month long Scout Ranger training that required us to experience a series of actual combat encounters before being allowed to graduate. There was no getting around this requirement. As they say in Scout Ranger school, *"Every SR student must smell the pungent odor of death and feel the agony of fear in a brutal environment, but still come out of it unscathed and a better person – an exemplary soldier who can be depended upon by his unit and comrades at any time."*

During our SR Class' Combat Test Mission, one SR classmate of mine was killed in action (KIA) and several others were wounded in action (WIA). Feeling more than sadness, we were proud of them. They fought gallantly and to us Scout Rangers, that is an honor – to fight and die in battle with our boots on.

The rigorous Spartan-like training of the Rangers is designed to make a fierce warrior out of an ordinary soldier. We are the only unit trained to shoot a target, the size of a tennis ball, held by our respective buddies at 25 meters. It is emotionally challenging to shoot a target in that kind of setup. Philippine military history, however, validates the accomplishments of the Scout Rangers. It is no secret that the FSRR has the highest number of Medal of Valor recipients. That medal is the highest combat award in the whole AFP.

The Scout Rangers have been proven to be reliable in past battles and will continue to be strong defenders of our freedom. They certainly proved it once again in the brutal 5-month-long Battle of Marawi in 2017.

The everyday grind of Scout Ranger training could never be understood by anyone who has not gone through it. But to those initiated, they will always have a soft spot in their hearts for Scout Ranger adventures and most naturally, will always have a huge smile on their faces whenever they remember and share their stories. The same is true with other special units.

The part of my training as a Scout Ranger I will never forget is called the "Escape and Evasion", known by the troops as *"Echo-Echo."* It was a situation where we were supposed to be prisoners of war. It was intended for us to experience a glimpse of what to expect when and if we were captured by the enemy. At that time, I thought it was the stupidest thing to include in a training. But I eventually conceded that there was wisdom behind it. I just didn't appreciate it much back then.

There was a point in *"Echo-Echo"* when I was subjected to too much hardship – the details of which, of course, I could not divulge publicly. It was one of the most dreaded training activities. In the process of that particular training exercise, I was pushed to the limit by so much pain and discomfort that I blurted out, *"I'm going to kill all of you if I get out of this alive!"*

While the training exercise was one that is close-to-reality, the reality was this: The entire activity was just part of the tedious process of culling the boys from the men and every SR trainee must go through it, everyone must pass the crucible. How much more would we experience in real war? Admittedly, I appeared like a fool – and I was an officer!

I certainly didn't kill any of my Ranger instructors for they were just doing their jobs. In fact, many of them became my very good buddies and mentors later in the field. With some, I had fun playing '*basket-brawl*' too! Basket-brawl is a hybrid kind of basketball that Scout Rangers play with much passion and intensity to the point that some leave the court bloody or with broken bones. But interestingly enough, everyone always managed to smile after the game and celebrate via a couple of beers. That was crazy-fun indeed.

That particularly hard and very rough training activity, however, gave me perspective on how to understand pain and torture. It made me tougher, no doubt. Thinking about it now, I can't help but remember the torture and suffering of our Lord and Savior Jesus Christ for our sins. He didn't lash out against His torturers. He could even have commanded His angels to wipe them all off from the face of this earth. Yet, He chose not to because He had a mission – to save us from *our* sins and to conquer death. In *Isaiah 53:5 (NIV)*, written many centuries before Christ, it says,

"But He was pierced for our transgressions, He was crushed for our iniquities; the punishment that brought us peace was on Him, and by His wounds we are healed."

Blessed and Grateful

Despite my own failures – self-made or otherwise, I graduated from the PMA and became a Scout Ranger. I was not among the strongest, but I was able to endure one of the toughest military trainings in the world. I believed I just cruised all along in all my military pursuits, trying to simply survive each day. Looking back now, I'm in awe of everything that happened – and is happening – in my life.

Indeed, God had something special for me to do, and He was preparing me without me being fully aware of it most of the time. I thought I was just following my own selfish dreams, when in fact, God had been calling my attention all along. I seemed not to hear, or I was purposely not heeding it.

I am embarrassed to realize that I was so preoccupied with myself and my mundane dreams most of the time, that I was not even thinking of God anymore. Yes, I had been so arrogant with what I had and what I had professionally achieved. But here's what God has to say to my – or our – smugness:

> "If I were hungry I would not tell you, for the world is mine, and ALL (*emphasis mine*) that is in it." *(Psalm 50:12 NIV)*

Moreover,

> "For the wisdom of this world is foolishness in God's sight. As it is written: He catches the wise in their craftiness." *(1 Corinthians 3:19 NIV)*

I was following my own desires and ambitions but God used these to accomplish His purposes. God is sovereign.

Challenges Ahead

The new batch of Scout Rangers was expected to face dangerous challenges.

In the late 1990s, the ASG seemed to have lost focus. As Christopher Shay pointed out in his *TIME* magazine feature, the ASG members "started behaving more like a gang of well-armed bandits driven by greed, not creed." Indeed, they engaged in kidnapping, rape, drug trafficking, and other criminal activities.

On December 18, 1998, ASG founder and leader Abdujarak Janjalani was killed in an armed encounter against the joint-operatives of the PNP and Civilian Armed Forces Geographical Unit (CAFGU) under MSg Juanillo Tubil, also a Scout Ranger, in Barangay Tumakid, Lamitan City, Basilan. With this, Philippine National Police (PNP) Chief Director General Roberto Lastimoso stated, "I don't think any more threat from this group is possible, although we're not taking it lightly. The leadership of the Abu Sayyaf is gone, totally gone. There is nobody who can fill the shoes of Janjalani right now." He added in a *South China Morning Post* article that the ASG would "die a natural death because of the absence of a strong personality and leadership."

Director General Lastimoso's hopeful assessment, though, didn't happen. The ASG changed course and concentrated on kidnapping foreigners. They used the ransom money to fund operations and their recruitment efforts in local communities. Those from impoverished territories in Mindanao were easily lured by the ASG's promises of getting a salary, and other uncommon perks, for being part of the group.

This was the kind of "new enemy" that the country's armed forces would face. Since the ASG was known for hiding out in the jungles of Mindanao, it was inevitable that the Scout Rangers would face them. It was not something that could be avoided.

•••••

Basic Airborne Course CL 80-97. (L-R) Myself (#02) and Sam Yunque (#03)

52nd Foundation Anniversary of the First Scout Ranger Regiment. (L-R) Cpt Albert Baloloy, 1Lt Jeffrey Cauguiran (at the back), Cpt Ian Martinez (at the back), Cpt Nicolas Danao, and myself. (November 2002)

(L-R) Phil Fortuno, author of the bestselling book *"No Man Left Behind: A Story of Valor in the Battle of Marawi"*, myself, and Lt Col Sam Yunque – former Commander of the 1st Scout Ranger Battalion, FSRR, SOCOM, PA and the principal character of the book. (December 2018)

Coffee Moments with Albert Baloloy (December 2018)

The Authors in Chicago, USA.

CHAPTER 5

IN THE COMPANY OF HEROES

"Though I walk in the midst of trouble, you preserve my
life; you stretch out your hand against the wrath of my
enemies, and your right hand delivers me."

— Psalm 138:7 (ESV)

In 2000, the armed forces were in the middle of President Joseph
Estrada's "all out war" against the State-declared terrorists. The
ASG seemed to intensify their operations. They went on a
kidnapping spree. In July, TV evangelist Wilde Almeda of the
Jesus Miracle Crusade (JMC) and 12 of his followers are taken
hostage by the group.

By September, *The Economist* reported that Estrada "finally
lost his patience with kidnappers from the Abu Sayyaf" and he
ordered "an assault on the southern island of Jolo."

However, in 2001, Estrada's term was cut short by the EDSA
II or the second installment of the People Power Revolution,
which placed President Gloria Macapagal-Arroyo in power. As
the transition was going on, the international community was
still reeling from the mass abduction that the ASG pulled off in
Sipadan, Malaysia. The hostages were taken by the Al-Qaeda-
linked Abu Sayyaf Group and brought to Jolo.

The Scout Rangers were brought to Jolo to bulk up the operating units. I was the commander of 15SRC, which was part of that contingent.

On May 27, 2001, after a couple of months of hunting the Abu Sayyaf terrorist-kidnappers in Jolo, we were informed that another group of Abu Sayyaf terrorists took hostages from the Dos Palmas Resort in Palawan, a very beautiful island in the southwestern part of the Philippines. The hostages included 27 Filipino nationals and three Americans – Guillermo Sobero and the missionary couple Martin and Gracia Burnham. They were taken to the island of Basilan across the Sulu Sea.

On June 2, 2001, the terrorists brought the hostages south of Palawan and then to Basilan island. They eventually occupied the Dr. Jose Torres Memorial Hospital and St. Peter's Church Compound in Lamitan, Basilan hoping for a better negotiating position to demand ransom for the hostages they had taken. They encountered the Philippine military – which included newly-graduated students of a regular Scout Ranger Course Class 142-00 under Cpt Ruben Guinolbay, a member of PMA "*Bantay-Laya*" Class of 1994 and SR Class 122-94 – in what was later known as the Lamitan Siege.

In the wake of the Lamitan Siege, about half of the 30 hostages were able to free themselves in the ensuing chaos. Unfortunately, the Abu Sayyaf terrorists escaped with the remaining hostages. It was an unfortunate incident, and I did not like the outcome - especially the malicious accusations hurled against the military in the aftermath.

Anticipating the escalation of more hostilities, senior military commanders decided to move my unit from Sulu island to Basilan to augment the troops operating in that area as a consequence of the new kidnappings. The rescue operations lasted for a year, costing a lot of lives lost for the government forces, the terrorists, and civilians.

In the Midst of Heroes

I had been part of many major combat encounters against the Abu Sayyaf Group before and some of the encounters involved rescuing hostages.

One of the most brutal combat encounters we had was in Balatanay, Isabela, Basilan on October 7, 2001. We had walked the whole night in order to hit the objective given to us by intelligence sources. According to the information, Abu Sayyaf commanders Khadaffy Janjalani, Hamisaraji Salih, Isnilon Hapilon, and Abu Sabaya led the group that we were going after. We thought they may have the hostages. But whether they did or didn't, we would always answer the call of duty. We always gave our best in every mission. This meant "paying the ultimate sacrifice" if the situation called for it.

On that day, we were operating with the troops under the irrepressible Cpt Harold *"Bullseye 6"* Cabunoc, who was the commander of the 10SRC, and Cpt Montano *"Rambo 6"* Almodovar, the Operations Officer of the 1SRB. Cpt Almodovar fought with me just a year before during the All-Out War in Matanog, Maguindanao. Both officers are members of PMA *"Bantay-Laya"* Class of 1994 and SR Class 121-95. They were heroes in many combat encounters. They are now Lieutenant Colonels and are still actively defending the freedom of our country.

To fight alongside known soldier-warriors is both an honor and privilege. I got to learn a lot from them, aside from being inspired. It was a rewarding experience to be with men who had fully embraced the military profession and everything that it entails. I could proudly say they were men who truly believed in the nobility of the profession of arms and that they sincerely adhere to what General Charles de Gaulle of France once said about "Military Professionalism",

> "Men who adopt the profession of arms, submit of their own free will to the law of perpetual constraint of their

own accord. They resist their right to live where they choose, to say what they think, to dress as they like, it needs but an order to settle them from their own family and dislocate their normal lives.

In the world of command, they must rise, march, run, endure bad weather, go without sleep or food, be isolated in some distant post, work until they drop. They ceased to be the master of their own fate. If they drop in their tracks, if their ashes are scattered to the four winds, that is all part and parcel of their job."

The two gentlemen would later make waves for themselves in the military in later years. Lt Col Cabunoc rose to become the commander of 33rd Infantry (*Makabayan*) Battalion in Central Mindanao and led his unit to be the reputable primary facilitator of peace and development - while battling terrorists and other lawless elements simultaneously - in their area of responsibility from 2017 to 2019. Lt Col Almodovar, on one hand, would outstandingly lead the 3rd Scout Ranger (*Excelsior*) Battalion deep behind enemy lines in the five-month long brutal Battle of Marawi in 2017 against ISIS-inspired terrorists.

Warriors at Work

We started to traverse the tropical jungle in darkness sometime past midnight. We walked all night struggling with fatigue and sleepiness. Before the first light of day, we rested for a bit and observed the mountainous and heavily vegetated surroundings. Our senses were heightened despite the lack of sleep and the discomfort. We knew that, as we observed the target area for any sign of the enemy, they were also monitoring us, observing their surroundings, and looking for us.

Soaked with dew and perspiration, some of the troops undid the buttons of their uniforms to relieve their heat and exhaustion. The brigade of assorted insects and other creatures in the jungle bothered us constantly. There were mosquitoes, leeches, and others that I didn't even recognize. I had been around these insects for such a long time, but I never seemed to have gotten used to their presence and "show of affection." They were fond of biting our exposed skin, so intimate with their buzzes and stings. *"Perks and privileges of operating in the tropical jungles"*, I thought in jest.

At about 6:30 A.M., Cpt Cabunoc communicated through the radio that we would be descending towards the shore where houses were sighted. He was the commander of the leading troops and I was the commander of the troops behind them.

He said, *"Jordan 6, this is Bullseye 6, over."*

"This is Jordan 6, go ahead, over." I responded.

"Jordan 6, prepare to move. We will be moving downward. Houses were sighted but no identified movements so far, over."

"Bullseye 6, wilco, over."

My troops and I made eye contact amongst ourselves and relayed messages via hand signals. Everybody was automatically on his feet with his heavy pack and ammunition-filled bandoleer. I suddenly thought, *"It would be nice to lie down in bed and sleep all day."* I looked around and speculated, *"Hmmm, I think my companions are thinking the same, but we must take care of this extraordinary business first."* So we got up and started walking in file formation silently and tactically.

After about 30 minutes of painstaking and tactical-descent towards the houses, Cpt Cabunoc called me over the radio and gave updates for coordination purposes.

"Jordan 6, Bullseye 6."

"This is Jordan 6, go ahead, over.

"Jordan 6, we are now slowly approaching a cluster of abandoned houses. Be ready to fight. I can sense the inevitable", said Bullseye 6 over the radio.

Suddenly, a barrage of gunfire was heard.

Brrrrrttttt!!! Boom!! Kablaammm!!

The sound of the lethal, uncoordinated, and out-of-tune war orchestra was at it again! Bullseye 6 and his Rangers were "warmly welcomed" with hot lead by the enemy while closing in on a cluster of seemingly-abandoned houses!

We responded with equal force. All hell broke loose! The deafening exchange of gun fire reverberated in the jungle. A new unusual fireworks display had began.

"Jordan 6, maneuver your troops to the right, over."

Bullesye 6 directed me to outflank the enemy to the right by occupying a tactically advantaged position and close in on the enemy position.

"Copy, sir!"

By that time, the disorienting smell of gunpowder had already dominated the air. Everyone tried to get the best position possible in the raging firefight.

As we rushed downward and maneuvered to the right of the leading troops, we were met by a volley of gun fire and rifle grenades from higher ground. We estimated it was about 75 meters from our position. We quickly dropped to the ground and looked for good cover. The enemy was relentless!

Hell-bent on outdoing the enemy, we managed to counter fire and interchangeably provided suppressive fires so other troops could find better defensive positions. We also communicated by hand signals to effectively determine the exact location of the enemy and also to avoid compromising our radio communication.

Cpt Cabunoc gave me another order, *"Jordan 6, move forward to my location, over."*

"Copy, sir", I quickly replied.

The battle raged on. The deafening barrage of gun fire and grenades continued for what seemed to be forever.

"Bullseye 6, Jordan 6, over. We are confronting heavy enemy fire from the high ground to our right, over!"

Suddenly, Cpt Almodovar was heard on the radio. *"Bullseye 6, Rambo 6, over! I will maneuver and occupy the high ground right of Jordan 6."*

The exchange of fire was steadily getting heavier by the minute. It appeared there was no end in sight soon. The chaotic combat situation had opened the door to more brutality.

After some time, which we curiously did not even notice, Cpt Almodovar was heard on the radio. *"Jordan 6, high ground occupied and secured, over!"*

The enemy fighters who were on the high ground had retreated upon the fierce assault of Cpt Almodovar and his troops.

"Bullseye 6, Jordan 6, this is Rambo 6, over. We got the high ground to your right, over"

"Yes!" I breathed to myself immediately upon hearing the reassuring radio messages of *Rambo 6*. Then after a while, close air support came and started pounding identified enemy positions with bombs and rockets. Watching the deadly 'fireworks' brought upon by the Air Force pilots, I wondered how many families would again suffer with the loss of their fathers, husbands, sons, brothers, uncles in the battlefield.

Though temporary, I felt a sigh of relief amid the chaos. It was a feeling worth a thousand relaxing full-body massages. That kind of combat relief was almost like the smell of the sweet aroma of my favorite coffee brewing.

We took advantage of the situation to eat some rice we cooked the night before we left the camp. Since we couldn't leave our respective battle positions, the Tail Scout, responsible for keeping our cooked rice, divided the hardened rice, and passed it around by "throwing" fist-sized cold-rice to every Ranger. Each of us tried "catching" small portions of it. It was the best tasting rice I've ever eaten in my jungle days! We had not eaten since the night we left our camp, so it was a very satisfying moment for us. Precious food indeed.

War Buddies

Rambo 6 had once again lived up to his reputation. I recalled his combat exploits when we were together way back in 1997 to 1999, as we fought together against local communist fighters in the mountains of the Southern Tagalog region and Mindoro Island. During the All-Out War in Maguindanao in 2000, he was also the commander of 17SRC that finished off the firefight after I had been wounded in that encounter.

For his part, Cpt Cabunoc did not seem to run out of fierceness in the thick of the battle. He audaciously led his men in clearing one house after the other. It was amazing to see him and his troops systematically clearing every nook and cranny of every house along our line of attack while we supported them. I said to myself, *"Lord, thank you for surrounding me with these men of valor. I couldn't ask for better war buddies than them."*

The leading troops steadily gained ground as the enemy-fighters started to withdraw. My troops moved forward alongside Cpt Cabunoc's. When we reached the suspected main battle position of the enemy, we hastily assaulted it with our guns blazing and us shouting at the top of our lungs with the intent of confusing the enemy, or making them think that we had gone suicidal and that there was no stopping a bunch of crazy-gung-ho soldiers like us.

It was a bloody mess as our troops and the enemy outgunned each other. Each wanted to beat the other to the draw, sending them to kingdom come the fastest.

After more than 6 hours of heavy fighting with more or less 100 enemy-fighters, everyone was accounted for. There were 17 Scout Rangers wounded in action, but no one was in a serious condition. We learned later from intelligence sources that 15 enemy-fighters were killed and 21 others were wounded. We recovered an M60E3 light machine gun (LMG) that the enemy hurriedly left in the bullet-riddled mosque. Evidently, they had tried to make the mosque their defensive position because it was made of concrete. From the mosque, we also recovered assorted types of ammunition and numerous items with high military intelligence value.

Before dusk, and through effective radio communication and coordination, we declared the immediate vicinity of the encounter site secured after a thorough and synchronized clearing operation. Now we could rest, and possibly get back to camp for a refreshing shower, hot meals, and even ice-cold beers – a luxury and a dream for every soldier after every bloody battle.

Merciful God

In the aftermath of the battle, fatigue and hunger were all over our faces. I had a throbbing headache. The long exposure to the elements, the on-edge emotions and most of all, the brutality of the whole thing had taken their toll on me.

We tried to eat some rice and canned sardines we had packed the night before. This time, without hiding from the bullets of the enemy, unlike what we did during the firefight. *"Food never tasted this good,"* I imagined. Gratitude filled my heart. I thought: *"We are alive...and eating the best locally-manufactured canned-sardines we could afford!"*

That was one of the bloodiest encounters that I experienced – next to what I went through the year before in Matanog, Maguindanao where I was seriously wounded and almost died. Both these encounters were close calls. I did not have any inkling of what God had in store for me in the days and years to come.

"Because he loves me, says the Lord, I will rescue him; I will protect him, for he acknowledges my name." *Psalms 91:14 (NIV)*

I thought, *"I don't even love Him as I should. I also didn't acknowledge Him as I ought to."* He is just plainly gracious, merciful, forgiving, and faithful. He continued to try to get my attention, and was overwhelmingly forbearing with me.

"If we are faithless, He will remain faithful, for He cannot disown himself." *2 Timothy 2:13 (NIV)*

I was in awe of God's greatness and his amazing grace.

•••••

"Boodle Fight". A unique, military tradition of eating together and sharing food as a manifestation of brotherhood. It is also a way of celebrating special occasions and victories (December 2002)

Surrounded by Warriors. I was at the center holding a Steyr AUG 5.56mm Assault Rifle (2001)

Victory Pose. In front of us was the M-60 machine gun recovered from the Abu Sayyaf terrorists in the Battle of Balatanay (October 2001)

After Battle Interview. With Captain Harold *"Bullseye 6"* Cabunoc, answering questions from a group of news correspondents (October 2001)

Heroes of Candelaria, Quezon. (L-R) With my former 9SRC Commanding Officer, the late Cpt Dennis Bumanglag (PMA '91), 1Lt Montano Almodovar (PMA '94), and myself.

CHAPTER

THE RESCUE

"You did not choose me, but I chose you and appointed
you to go and bear fruit, fruit that remains,
so that whatever you ask the Father in my name
he will give you."

— John 15:16 (NET Bible)

I was watching with gusto the 2002 NBA Western Conference
Finals between the Los Angeles Lakers and Sacramento Kings
when I got the orders to deploy to Zamboanga del Norte for
another mission. Enjoying a respite from non-stop combat
operations was heaven-on-earth for an infantryman like me. And
come to think of it, I was watching live NBA game on cable TV!
Ecstasy indeed.

To have a dish cable in the remote area of Basilan was a fancy
thing for us back then. It gave us a great respite from a year of
continuous combat operations as we tried to neutralize the Abu
Sayyaf terrorists, and rescue the remaining hostages that had
been captive for a year by this time.

The year 2002 seemed to be the year for Chris Webber, Vladé
Divac, and the Sacramento Kings. But Kobe Bryant, Shaquille
O'Neal, and the Lakers were playing the best of their careers.
The Lakers went on to become the 2002 NBA Champions. The
U.S. Army Special Forces servicemen cross training with us
were so amazed to see Kobe and Shaq posters in the receiving

area of my barracks. They were puzzled by our enthusiasm for basketball. They were wondering how in the world we embraced this sport which was invented by a Canadian-American minister named Dr. James Naismith.

Our U.S. Special Forces counterparts were bigger, taller and more muscular. They loved American football. However, basketball was the only sport we played and we had a concrete basketball court in the middle of our camp with a huge logo of the "Musang", a local panther we used as a symbol for the Scout Rangers. We always played competitively with our US counterparts during our spare time.

It's funny when I recollect about those games. Their athletic prowess never really helped. They have good basketball players in the contingent but none among those stationed with us. They played basketball with passion like they play football, and losing seemed to get on their nerves and get the worst out of them a lot of times.

But as for me, *"Winning is only second to the love of the game itself."* Most of the time, we got the "second" part. That pissed them off.

In those hotly contested games, they never won until they left our camp to go back to the United States. They were so good in a lot of things but not in everything. I thought, *"We really cannot have everything in this life."*

In the field, or 'in-country' as some may call it, the cable TV was a great diversion for the troops to kill boredom when not in combat operations. I was recuperating from some blisters acquired after many days in the jungle. Traversing the tropical jungles with combat boots on for many days was very challenging. Sand, soil particles, and water would get inside our boots as we crossed rivers, streams and mountains. This would create friction on our feet and eventually destroy the integrity of the skin. We usually put on petroleum jelly to protect our feet but that can only do so much. I requested Lt Col Reynato Padua, my battalion commander in the 1st Scout Ranger *(Unbeatable)* Battalion and who is also a member of PMA *"Matikas"* Class of 1983 and SR Class 49-83, to allow me to rest and give time for my blisters to heal.

Our Battalion had been deployed to Zamboanga del Norte just a week earlier. 1SRB was composed of the following companies: 1SRC led by 1Lt Jeffrey *"Jepoy"* Cauguiran, who fought with me in the All Out War in Matanog, Maguindanao two years earlier as an Executive Officer of 18SRC; 10SRC led by my classmate 1Lt Albert *"Bert"* Baloloy; 12SRC led by 1Lt Enrico *"Boix"* Dingle, a member of PMA *"Mabikas"* Class of 1996 and SR Class 131-97; 15SRC led by my Ex-O 1Lt John Andrada; and Sniper CL 03-02 led by Cpt Isagani Criste, a member of PMA *"Bantay-Laya"* Class of 1994 and SR Class 121-94.

The terrorists brought the remaining hostages in that area hoping for better negotiations, away from the influence of the US intelligence that the Philippine military were getting. The Visiting Forces Agreement (VFA) limited the American military presence in the island of Basilan and Zamboanga City.

Joint Military Training Exercises dubbed as *"Balikatan,"* a Filipino term for shoulder to shoulder, were regularly held. That year, Basilan was the site for obvious military reasons. The terrorists were well aware of the American government aiding the Philippine military in terms of technical intelligence capability. They thought they could negotiate well in that area away from American influence meddling with the negotiation process.

My company was led by my Executive Officer, 1Lt John Andrada – a member of Philippine Army Officer Candidate School (PA OCS) Class 16-97 and SR Class 142-01 – when they joined the contingent near Zamboanga del Norte. I was hoping for a resolution soon, and praying that all the hostages would be freed; that the Burnham Couple would be home to the US, and that the soldiers could go to see their families. As I pondered much on the possible outcomes of our mission, unpleasant memories came rushing back. I remembered those who offered the ultimate sacrifice. I imagined the fatherless and the widows who would be facing the challenges of life without their husbands. In that area, beheadings are regular occurrences. Over the years, terrorists had mutilated their hostages as well as civilians who were not supportive of them. The Abu Sayyaf bandits and their supporters had become synonymous with brutality.

On June 5, 2002, I got a message from the radio room. My Battalion Commander, Lt Col Padua, ordered me to proceed to Zamboanga del Norte. He instructed me to join my unit the next day. Transportation by land and air would be coordinated. At that moment, I wished the Rescue Mission was already over. Looking at my blisters, I took a deep breath. They were almost healed but my emotions were not. Patriotism within me made me want to be with my men and finish the mission but the temptation to keep myself out of that chaos was also present. With a heavy heart, I packed my gear. I reminded myself, commanders should lead until the end – no undue excuses - even with blistered feet. Basketball can wait, so let's go and rock 'n roll with the troops!

Retreat to Zamboanga del Norte

There were a lot of AFP units in this operation coined as "Operation Daybreak". The Scout Rangers, who had been operating non-stop from Central and Northwestern Mindanao to Sulu and Basilan islands, were designated as supporting effort. The Marines were with the main effort.

Intelligence information stated that Abu Sabaya and his group, together with the hostages, were sighted somewhere in *Triple "S"* – short for Siocon, Sirawai and Sibuco municipalities of Zamboanga del Norte. Accordingly, they had been forced to leave Basilan island due to the massive and relentless combat military operations initiated by the Philippine Army's 103rd Infantry Brigade under the leadership of then Colonel Hermogenes

Esperon Jr., a member of PMA *"Marangal"* Class of 1974. Colonel Esperon would later rise to become the AFP Chief of Staff in 2006, Presidential Adviser on the Peace Process in 2008, and the Chief of the Presidential Management Staff in 2009 all under the administration of former President Gloria Macapagal-Arroyo. On May 23, 2016, he was appointed by President Rodrigo Roa Duterte to be his National Security Adviser.

The downfall of Abu Sabaya started after the capture by the military – particularly by the 1st Scout Ranger Battalion – of the ASG's vaunted stronghold Camp Abdurrajak in Puno Mohaji, Isabela, Basilan on April 30, 2000. Puno Mohaji is within the so-called Sampinit Complex, which is part of Basilan National Park where other mountains like Mt. Abong-abong, Hill 800 and Basilan Peak are located. The area became a favorite lair and refuge of the ASG away from the reach of government forces because of its dense jungle and rugged terrain.

•••

I was picked up by a UH-1H Huey helicopter going to Zamboanga del Norte. To my surprise, I was the only passenger. I felt so special because I had never experienced this before! The combat pilot happened to be my PMA classmate, Captain Larry Pine, a distinguished fighter pilot of the Philippine Air Force (PAF). Cpt Pine is now scaling new heights as an international commercial pilot.

We arrived in the landing zone – where a lot of AFP units were consolidating – at about 3:00 P.M., I was told by the officer-in-charge that I would be transported by a convoy of mechanized troops which included the Marine Force Recon – an elite unit that fought with me two years earlier during the All-Out War in Central Mindanao where I was wounded. At about 4:40 P.M., we jumped off.

After an hour, I was dropped off and eventually linked-up with my company. I felt so at home with my soldiers. They were enjoying each other's company and were willing to fight alongside each other to accomplish the mission. Only now do I realize that we gave all without thinking that we were compensated to an equivalent of 400 USD at that time. In tears, I remember those who offered their lives as well as those who are still in active military service continuing to fight for the freedom of our country to this day. Many of my fellow soldiers and good friends paid a high price so that others can live peacefully in the comforts of their homes with their families.

After more than sixteen years since that day, one of my men talked with me on the phone. He could still vividly remember the exact words I spoke that afternoon when I arrived to encourage them. After admitting they were dead-tired and their morale was already running low after walking in rugged terrain for days during all kinds of weather conditions, he told me that the words I uttered that time motivated them to carry on. I was speechless when I learned that. I had no idea the words I told my troops deeply connected with them back then, and had been one of their tipping points. Indeed, we don't often realize the power of positive and reinforcing words. God sent who was needed at the right time in order to encourage and motivate our fellow men.

Surveying our harboring position situated on a high ground overlooking a logging road, I thought to myself, "*Only God knows when we are going to get out of here alive and in one piece.*" I prayed we all could.

Green Light

I woke up at dawn and observed our defensive positions. It was amazing to have this inner confidence and assurance that we have relieving sentinels throughout the night. Having an omnipotent God and sentinels who never sleep on posts are such formidable protection. Who could ask for more?

Scout Rangers are used to having watchmen all night. We were trained to fight sleepiness and fatigue during our watch. Failure to do so could mean everyone losing his life. It's mind-boggling for an ordinary civilian to comprehend how we do things in the jungle, especially at night. Being with those valiant warriors was an experience of a lifetime.

At about 7:00 A.M., one of my men brought two Dacon Logging employees to my location. *"Sir, nakakita sila ng mga bakas ng paa at naiwang tsinelas sa logging road habang papunta sila sa trabaho* [Sir, these men saw footprints and a broken slipper along the logging road while they were on their way to work]." Thoughts hastily raced in my mind. *"Could it be the Abu Sayyaf who carelessly crossed the road during the night? If so, they are not that far from us."*

To answer the questions in my mind, one of the two men presented to me was Bernardo Reseroni, the father of Edwin Reseroni, who was one of the hostages that the terrorists kidnapped on June 2. According to Bernardo, *"Kilala ko ang tsinelas at ballpen na yan. Sa anak ko yan* [I recognize those slippers and ballpen. They belong to my son]", as he pointed to the slippers and ballpen recovered by one of my Rangers along one of the trails in the area.

"Hooaah! This is a breakthrough!" I nearly exclaimed. The logging road was about 300 meters from our location. We had to see the footprints! I packed up and brought a seven-man team with me. We rushed downhill towards the logging road as the rest of the troops packed up. We did not eat our breakfast because we felt the urgency to move quickly. As soon as I saw the tracks, I had the feeling *"this is it!"*

Within minutes, the troops were battle-ready and everyone was quiet, sensing something was about to happen soon. We always get that kind of feeling with every upcoming combat engagement.

"Establish contact with the Tactical Command Post", I instructed Ranger Dennis Bugayong, my radioman who is a member of SR Class 135-99. As soon as I got my Battalion Commander on the

line, I gave the details of the situation and the new information that we got. He instructed me to hang on for a bit as he asked for advice from the Task Force commander for further instructions.

"Jordan 6, this is Unbeatable 6 (Lt Col Padua), over."

"Go ahead, sir", I replied on the radio.

"Stay put, Jordan 6. Adjacent units will be directed towards your area. Don't move until further orders from me!", Lt Col Padua instructed.

"Sanamagan!", I mumbled.

I thought, *"All this time, we always have problems looking for the enemy. And now, the fresh tracks are right here. I'm not letting them slip away this time."* My Ex-O, Platoon Sergeant and team leaders were all looking at me. They were awaiting my decision. From their eyes they were sort of saying, *"Damn! We go for this, sir. This is what we have been looking for more than a year already!"*

I grabbed the radio handset from my radioman.

"Unbeatable 6, this is Jordan 6, over."

"Go ahead Jordan 6, over."

I politely and clearly explained to my Battalion Commander why we should not stay put. I respectfully recommended that while adjacent units were closing in, we should start tracking the enemy because any passing moment was so crucial. We might easily lose them in a heavily vegetated tropical jungle like this. I didn't want to be labeled as an unduly assertive junior officer but I deemed it necessary at that time to make my point crystal clear. We needed to seize that rare moment.

After a while, Lt Col Padua agreed. I assumed the blessing or green light was given by MGen Glicerio *"Glykes"* Sua, our Task Force Commander who is also a member of PMA *"Masigasig"* Class of 1972 and SR Class 15-72. As soon as I got the "go signal" I gathered the troops except for those who were on perimeter guard duties. I told my men, *"Ihanda ang sarili. Ngayon na 'to."* ["Brace yourselves. This will be the day."] Then we prayed,

> "He who dwells in the shelter of the Most High will rest in the shadow of the Almighty. I will say of the Lord, He is my refuge and my fortress, my God, in Whom I trust... You will not fear the terror of the night, nor the arrow that flies by day...Because He loves me, says the Lord, I will rescue him. I will protect him, for he acknowledges my name." *Psalm 91: 1-2, 5, 14*

I concluded, *"In Jesus' Name, all the Rangers say"* and everybody responded in controlled voices, *"Amen!"*

Psalm 91, referred to by its Latin title *"Qui habitat"*, is known as the Psalm of Protection commonly invoked in times of hardship. The Scout Rangers pray this prayer every time we go for battle. It is amazing how each of us prayed this prayer with sincerity, even though some of us were not really certain of our faith.

Looking back, how I wished I could have been an instrument for them to know, on a personal level, our Lord and Savior Jesus Christ. But back then I was also struggling with my faith. I didn't feel I had that spiritual maturity to share my faith deeply because I was not even living my life in obedience to Him.

Combat Tracking at its Finest

Before our movement to continue tracking the enemy from where we talked to the two Dacon employees, I was informed by Lt Col Padua that 10SRC led by Cpt Albert Baloloy, who was about one kilometer map distance from us, would close in to our position and provide us with supporting effort. Hearing the name of my snappy PMA classmate, Cpt Baloloy, put a smile on my face. I knew I could rely on him for support. As certain as night and day, he would run to hell and back anytime even if it would be a marathon to nowhere just to back me up.

We started our movement at about 7 A.M. together with one squad of Sniper Class 03-02, composed of four personnel led by Ranger Marchan Diawan – a member of SR Class 132-97 - who was placed under my tactical control (TACON). The tracks led us to the creek. I instructed my Ex-O to lead a 14-man section to traverse the high ground on the right side of the creek. I brought with me my Platoon Sergeant, Ranger Cirilo *"Jagger"* Jagmoc – a member of SR Class 71-85, and my 14-man section plus. I anticipated an imminent combat encounter as soon as we reached the bed of the creek. I thought, *"This will be a bloody and difficult confrontation."*

There was not much space to maneuver or to take cover in order to be concealed. We didn't have much choice but to follow the creek and see for ourselves what lies in it. I told my Ex-O that if we were caught up in a messy situation at the creek, at least he could still provide the second force to finish the job. He would also serve as our contact with our Battalion TCP in case we were pinned down.

As soon as we hit the creek, we saw a lot of the enemy's tracks all over the place. These footprints were really fresh. I imagined they were just several meters ahead of us. We moved in a tactical manner, which meant we moved slowly and very carefully not to alert the enemy of our presence. We avoided old tree branches, rocks, or anything that might create any noise. Stepping on dead tree branches was inevitable. The cracking sounds seemed to be intensified even if it actually wasn't loud. Our senses no doubt were heightened. High levels of caution would work to our advantage right now.

At about 9 A.M., we found a hammock, several medicines and personal belongings. The possibility of an imminent encounter was felt by everyone. We'd been through these situations before.

Our movements were drowned in the mixed sounds of water flowing from the creek and tweeting birds. The unpredictable terrain and heavy vegetation were so challenging. Sharp leaves and tree branches scratched our faces and exposed skin. After about more than an hour of stealthily stalking the enemy, *"Anak ng tipaklong!* ["Son of a grasshopper!]"*, my lead scout mumbled as he approached me.

"Anyare? [What happened?]"*, I asked.

"Nawala ang bakas, sir [We lost the tracks, sir]"*, replied my lead scout.

"Anak ng...! [Son of ...!]"*

I almost shouted with a curse as well. It was a good thing that I came to my senses quickly and remembered I was responsible for the lives of these men. I thought, *"I'd better maintain my composure."* We stopped for a while and studiously examined the surroundings.

At about 11 AM, *"Bingo!"*, whispered my lead scout, Ranger Tamayo, as he gave me the thumbs up and a wide grin on his face.

I always smiled at Ranger Glen *"Cocoy"* Tamayo's antics and superstitions. I teasingly called him "K-9", alluding to the outstanding tracking skills of a canine using its senses. Ranger Tamayo's tracking skill was impressive to say the least. In fact, I always highlight his extraordinary skill whenever I'm invited to speak and tell the story. People are always amused when I describe him. Always, 100 percent all the time. As much as I am proud of him, I am also filled with sadness because he died a senseless death two weeks after the rescue.

The footprints and mud markings were covered by the enemy with old coconut leaves, probably done by the last man in their battle formation in order to hide their tracks. But his jungle survival skills were no match for my ever-focused and deadly lead scout.

The Abu Sayyaf bandits were considered to be well-versed in guerilla fighting. They had lived in the jungle for years and had almost mastered every trick and deception thought of in jungle fighting. They were shrewd fighters, aside from being ruthless. The only possible problem for them would be that Zamboanga del Norte was not their playground. Like us, they were new to the area. To be effective, the terrorists would have to adapt faster than we did to their environment, otherwise they would soon be statistics on our battle scoreboard.

Closing In

We continued to follow the footprints, which became prominent again as these tracks led us to high ground. As we reached the top of the hill, we discovered a farm. And to our surprise and delight, leftovers of *nangka* (jackfruit), *marang*, and coconut were all over the place. We saw foot markings on the trunks of the trees. "*They were so hungry*", I said. "*They had a feast*", my radioman pitched in. We did not spend much time at the farm. We knew the urgency, we needed to move fast, and think faster.

I figured that, at the way we were moving, the enemy might have gained some distance so I hand-signaled to the troops to move faster. At this time, the troops of 1Lt Andrada had consolidated with us.

As we moved along, we noticed the consistent sight of chewed coconut meat. We were not certain whether the terrorists did that out of stupidity not knowing its implications or one of the hostages was actually doing it intentionally. "*Good! Keep up your stupidity and we will soon be up to your ass*", I said to myself confidently.

At the end of the ridge, about 100 meters away from where they ate their breakfast, the tracks led us downward towards a big river. I sensed danger. I deployed my troops utilizing our Scout Ranger SOPs. We stayed low using the combination of bounding overwatch and crawling. After 15 minutes of doing so, we discovered that they were not there. They had already left. *"They are not that far."* I thought. They were really hungry as evidenced by their debris. They harvested every wild fern they could find and every fruit-bearing tree that they passed by.

At about 12:15 P.M., I could feel fatigue and hunger. We had not eaten our breakfast yet. I looked at the faces of my troops struggling with the heavy weight of their backpacks. Inside them were rations of rice and sardines plus the ammunition-filled pouches that hung on their bandoleers. We continued to move in silence. I raised my hand in a closed fist, which meant to halt. I gave instructions that we would be eating our lunch as fast as we could. We could not afford to waste time because we would lose the enemy tracks. We saw the heavy clouds forming and knew the possibility that rain might happen soon.

After about 15 minutes, everyone was done eating and just waiting for instructions to resume the movement. Rice and sardines had never tasted that good, especially when one's sugar level had been going south due to hunger and exhaustion. I observed the surroundings and analyzed the terrain ahead. I noticed some of my men dozed as they leaned over their backpacks. The crash and burn of low blood sugar or hypoglycemia can induce sleepiness and loss of focus. Fatigue and exhaustion had also moved in.

"Prepare to move," I commanded in a whisper.

My team leaders relayed my instruction via hand signals. Immediately, the troops rose up like camels with their heavy backpacks, bandoleers, and gear hoisted on their tired bodies.

We continued the slow tactical movement while carefully focusing on the footprints we were following. At about 1:30 P.M., the footprints started to lead us northeast towards a mountain with a steep 45-degree slope.

At about 2 P.M., it started to drizzle.

As happy as I was that Mother Nature gifted us with "Ranger weather" – any inclement weather condition is Ranger weather because we thrive in it – I was also apprehensive that the rain would eventually erase the footprints. All our efforts since early morning would be in vain. It would be a significant setback for us.

The terrain was very challenging, rocky and slippery with vegetation. The heaviness of our backpacks, ammunition-filled pouches, and other gear was aggravating the situation. I could see frustration in some of my men's faces. The discipline of keeping silent as part of the tactical movement, along with the urge to express their frustration, was like a balloon that was about to burst any time. Some of them slipped as they struggled on the unstable rocks and the wet ground and surroundings. Some slid towards the person they followed as they walked in file. A rifle here and there would hit a rock when one of them would be knocked off and lose their balance. Our M60 machine gunners struggled with their heavy guns aggravated by the chain of bullets crisscrossing their bodies. I felt so frustrated too, but I didn't show it. My mind was so preoccupied with all the things that were at stake. Damn the body pains, exhaustion and what not! We were there to achieve something important, not to whine or to be preoccupied with sunny thoughts.

By 2:30 P.M., we hit the top of the ridge. It took about 10 minutes for everyone to reach the ridgeline. As soon as everyone was all accounted for, I contacted the Tactical Command Post to give updates on our location. I struggled as the drizzle erased the critical points drawn with markers on my map. We were soaked with combined sweat and drizzle. The heavy rain would soon pour. After relaying our location to the Command Post at approximately 2:50 P.M., I hand-signaled for everyone to get on their feet again.

The lead scout, Ranger Tamayo, had descended about five

meters when he suddenly signaled us to stop. Everyone slowly sank on their knees. Everyone knew something was afoot. I went forward to see what Ranger Tamayo saw. He then pointed his hands to a direction. There was a blue-colored makeshift tent!

Bingo!

My lead scout and I looked at each other. We both knew what the other was thinking. We both anxiously smiled a bit, confident that it was something significant.

Tactically, we began crawling forward to take a good look. The slope was so steep – about 45 to 60 degrees in variation. We communicated by hand signals and I gathered that there were four tents approximately 20 meters from our location with hammocks underneath. Those were the only ones we could barely see. There were small unstable rocks and the ground was very slippery due to the early drizzle that had by now become light rain. If we crawled farther, we might have slipped and fallen, or cause the small rocks to fall towards the location of the blue-colored tents, effectively compromising our position and alerting the enemy.

Instantly, I crawled back to my previous position and summoned 1Lt Andrada, the two platoon sergeants, and five team leaders to brief them of the situation. I contacted the TCP to give an initial update. I tried my very best to draw our battle positions on the wet ground. We agreed to send a section led by Ranger Jagmoc to the right portion of the target area descending towards the creek. The section of Ranger Bustanera under the command of 1Lt Andrada would take the left portion of the target area and assume the skirmisher position.

The leading team of Ranger Radney Magbanua, a member of SR Class 129-97, would lead the way, along with our ace lead scout Ranger Tamayo. I positioned myself between Team 2 under Ranger Carlito San Pablo – a member of SR Class 115-94 - and Team 3 under Ranger Joel Dela Fuente – another member of SR Class 121-95 - to get a better position and control of the entire group of troops. Team 1 would reconnoiter so that the possibility of the enemy detecting our main body would be minimal or avoided when we decided to close in. The rest of the troops would occupy a skirmisher position and crawl to the point where they could no longer move forward due to the steep slope.

As everyone readied to proceed to their agreed positions, I contacted the TCP for updates. The adjacent units in the area – namely 10th SRC led by Cpt Albert Baloloy, Sniper Class 03-02 under 1Lt Lee Romero, who is a member of PMA "*Masinag*" Class of 1998 and SR Class 136-99, and 14th Scout Ranger "*Mabalasik*" Company under Cpt John Andres, also a PMA classmate of mine – had been instructed to move towards our location. They were all right now moving towards us. I assumed the choppers were flying over us to deploy troops. Good thing that these terrorists were so used to the sounds of choppers. They were not aware of our close proximity. Heavy rain started to fall as the reconnaissance section went their way. After some time, my radioman Ranger Bugayong handed me the hand set.

"*Jordan 6, Team 1, over.*" I could hardly hear the whisper. The heavy rain made it worse.

"*Jordan 6, go ahead, over.*"

"*Tatlong kalaban. Nilalaro ang ulan…galing sa tulo ng tolda… nakahiga sa duyan, over.*" ["Three armed-targets. Playing with rainwater…flowing from their tents…lying in their hammocks, over."]

I couldn't move towards their location as the space and terrain between us wouldn't allow it. I couldn't see what they saw from their location. Our vision was hindered by vegetation, heavy rain, and the geography of the vicinity. It was very challenging.

"*Pwede pa ba kayong lumapit para makalapit din kami* [Can you move closer to their position so we can close in as well]?",

I asked softly. I wanted them to precisely confirm what group we would be fighting soon. We needed to know and assess the situation as best as we could.

"*Wilco sir*", came the reply on the radio.

After some time, "*One-Zero…* [Ten meters]", a whisper from the other end.

"*Kumusta sighting? Makita nyo ba?* [How's the sighting? Can you see them?]", I queried.

"*Jordan 6, malabo, foggy, malakas ang ulan, over.* [Jordan 6, very poor…foggy…rain too heavy, over.]"

From our position, the fog was also impeding our visibility. I learned later that only four people could actually see the two blue tents with hammocks. They were Rangers Tamayo, Catague, Jagmoc and Rodelio Tuazon. From my location, I couldn't see the other tents that we had seen from the high ground. "*This is very hard,*" I mumbled. I realized, the rain and fog made it hard for us to get a good view of the enemy. On the other hand, these factors would give us an advantage in terms of cover and concealment which we badly needed at that time. Then, a very anxious voice came over the radio.

The leading team had inched forward so that they could have a better look. At about five meters from the enemy, they had found an elevated ground covered with foliage, barely enough to provide the cover and concealment they desperately needed.

"*Jordan 6, kinukuha ang baril…patingin-tingin…advise, over!* [Jordan 6, targets picked up their rifles…looking around… advise, over]."

The most forward elements I figured were in danger. "*Stay put… posisyon muna lahat…* [Stay put…allow others to position…]."

"Pull the trigger only when necessary", I instructed the radioman to relay to Ranger Jagmoc. I have been with Ranger Jagmoc for a long time and I trusted his judgment. He had served the Rangers for a long time and had gained even more combat experiences than I had. I just happened to be his commander.

Then a *"Bang!"* was heard.

I wasn't even able to finish my instructions when I heard two successive single-gunshots!

"Bang! Bang!"

Ranger Jagmoc hit the terrorist right on his forehead. Simultaneously, the two other Rangers picked their respective armed targets.

Bang! Bang!...Bang! Bang!

I knew from the kind of gunshots I had just heard that they were from my Rangers – two sets of crisp double-taps to the head and chest area. Clean shots always. My instruction was to "neutralize clear and armed targets only", and the armed enemy fighters moving dangerously too close to them were inarguably "clear and armed targets".

I would learn later that a huddle of enemy sentries saw Ranger Jagmoc and his buddies and quickly shot at them but missed. In response, the Rangers retaliated with double taps to the heads of the enemy fighters in their sight.

"Jordan 6, yari ang tatlo, over! [Jordan 6, 3 enemy targets down, over!]"

The deadly *musangs* were out!

Brrrrttt! Brrrrttt! Pak! Boom! Pak! Boom! Boom! came in the reply from the surprised enemy. We ducked for cover as the enemy fired at our general position indiscriminately. The enemy wasn't sure of my troops' exact positions.

By this time, I was not whispering into the radio anymore. I was shouting as I gave orders and directed my troops in the ensuing firefight. Suddenly a barrage of gun fire coming from the high ground, across our position, sent us scrambling for cover.

Bang! Bang! Boom! Boom! Brrrrttt! Kablam!

The gun fire almost hit us dead-center. The enemy already had a good idea of our primary position.

As the fighting was going on, Ranger Tamayo's rifle malfunctioned. To have a problem like that in the middle of a firefight is the worst thing that can happen. It is as if you have been left for dead! Seeing what was happening, Ranger Catague – a member of SR Class 143-01 - quickly provided Ranger Tamayo with cover fire. Ranger Tamayo instinctively grabbed the rifle of a dead enemy fighter and used it as his own weapon as he continued to engage the other terrorists.

We struggled to look for good cover as we adjusted our positions and returned fire. The enemy was hitting us from all angles. They had snipers posted on the high ground across our position.

Damn!

After a few seconds, *"Boom! Boom!"* became *"Zhing! Zhing!"* – which meant enemy rounds were very close to my head already! Combat veterans knew too well what *"Zhing! Zhing!"* does to anyone on its path. It brings only two things – serious injury or death.

Boom! A rifle grenade exploded in front of us, a good five meters away from me.

I lost my hearing for a few second as the enemy's rifle grenade exploded. Any minute I was anticipating feeling the pain and blood flowing from my body just like when I got hit two years earlier. I quickly ran my hands over my torso, feeling for something unusual. I felt no pain. *"I'm good! I was spared!"* What a miracle!

Ranger Abner Eustaquio – a member of SR Class 135-99 - who was beside me, was wailing in pain. Blood was oozing from his mouth. Scout Snipers Joe Lagadon and Jerry Pulmano - a member of SR Class 136-99 - on my right side, were also wounded. The M203 grenade exploded in front of us and all of them were wounded, except me. Team 1 had the largest number of casualties, namely: Rangers Radney Magbanua, Rene Mabilog, and Alvin Maddatu. Team 2's wounded were: Rangers Carlito San Pablo, Rodelio Tuazon – the designated medic of our group – and CAA Alejandro Ebo, who was our local guide. They continued to hold their lines as the fighting raged on.

"Jordan 5 (1Lt Andrada), *bugahan mo sa kabilang high ground, over!* [Jordan 5, deliver suppressive fire across the other high ground, over!]", I commanded.

"Wilco, sir. Right away!" came the prompt reply on the radio.

Although 1Lt Andrada could hear my voice as he was located not so far on the left side of our skirmisher formation, we both decided to follow SOP and use tactical radios, especially during firefights.

By that time, the firefight was at its peak. Guns of various calibers were in overdrive. Every weapon appeared to be trying to outdo the other. Different sounds emanated from various weapons, but all came bearing the same consequence, death – nothing more, nothing less.

Automatic machinegun fire from our troops was directed towards the high ground across from us where they were firing from. Enemy fire continued to barrage our positions, making us move from one position to the other, scrambling to find whatever cover we could find. What we did was to fire and maneuver, and we Rangers do it best.

Fire and maneuver – Scout Ranger School taught us that well. Anyone who remains static in a firefight will likely to be moved out in a body bag. But firing and maneuvering in the tight spot that we were in was not easy. We needed to do more. We adjusted, and returned fire, effectively using fire and maneuver. We got a little leverage, but the enemy were fiercely fighting back. They needed to survive and get out from the shit hole that we made for them. They wanted us to engage them indiscriminately, but we chose not to. My order to my troops was to selectively engage armed-targets only. I was always thinking of the hostages who were possibly with them at that time.

My troops knew well their tactical limitations. Hence, we fired in semi-automatic only as we tried to avoid sustained and indiscriminate firing. The site, where the blue-colored tent was located, was our main focus. I wanted to drive the enemy away from the tent and leave whoever was in there at that time.

To do that, I directed my troops to fire at the surrounding areas and neutralize identified enemy positions, particularly enemy snipers' nests. The concept was to isolate the tent area and demoralize the enemy, eventually forcing them to abandon it.

The intense battle raged for about 35 minutes. As the gunfire slowly died down to intermittent shots, we knew that it was an indication that the enemy had started to retreat from the fight.

"Jordan 6, Team 1 will assault, over!", Ranger Rey Maranan – another member of SR Class 135-99 - the Team 1 radioman informed us.

"Hold your fire! Team 1 will assault", I commanded the rest of my troops over the radio.

We held our fire while the composite Team 1 and Team 2 Rangers led by Ranger Jagmoc assaulted and closed in on enemy positions. As they advanced towards the enemy, three members of Team 1 and two from Team 2 were wounded. They were quickly pulled out from the firefight and evacuated to high ground secured by Team 3, which also had one casualty, under Ranger Dela Fuente.

As the firefight raged, Rangers Tamayo and Catague tactically maneuvered to the tent where they had earlier sighted fair-skinned persons. Slowly, they approached the target tent and saw an emaciated Gracia Burnham.

"*Who are you?*" asked Gracia.

"*We are the Scout Rangers! I'm Ranger Cocoy Tamayo, Philippine Army!*", Ranger Tamayo responded in broken English.

"*Oh my God! Thank God!*" Gracia exclaimed.

Some troops gathered the enemy's possesions and other war materiel as fast as they could, while others secured the area and kept focus on the surroundings. Ranger Catague discovered a few rounds of M203 inside one of the bags beside the hostages. We would later learn that the terrorists made Martin carry those along with other stuff to keep him burdened and slow-moving to dissuade him from escaping.

Within minutes, "*Jordan 6, nandito ang "box" (our code for the 'hostages')* [Jordan 6, the box (hostages) is here]", reported the radioman.

Quickly, I instructed 1Lt Andrada, "*Jordan 5, secure the area. Consolidate ang tropa, dalhin ang sugatan sa taas!*" ["Jordan 5, secure the area. Consolidate the troops, gather our wounded troops and bring them to the high ground!]"

Adjacent units were directed to block possible directions or routes of withdrawal. Tropical jungles are not easy to deal with. Adjacent units may only be 500 meters apart in map distance, but this is farther when translated to ground distance, considering barriers and other factors. It was so difficult for us to link up with each other in a short period of time. I couldn't even see my own troops during the firefight even when they were just meters away.

I rushed towards the stream bed, sliding on the muddy steep slope, bumping onto rocks and old tree branches. My radioman followed suit. He goes where I go. We were war-buddies.

The heavy rain turned into a drizzle. I was so grateful for the timing of the rain. It started and stopped when it mattered most.

As we reached the stream bed, I saw Gracia. She was hit in the leg. I gazed at the body of Martin. His shirt was soaked in blood and he looked so pale. From my combat experience, I knew Martin was in bad shape but I didn't want to further entertain that thought.

Yes, I was fighting the horrible reality of armed encounter. "*This cannot be*", I said to myself as I tried to deny the facts. I was so uncomfortable looking at Martin; but still, I thanked God for Gracia. She was wounded but alive. Another hostage, Edwin Reseroni, a logging company employee, escaped during the early stages of the encounter.

"*Sir, parang patay din ang isang babae* [Sir, I think the other lady is also dead]", whispered one of my men. He was referring to Ediborah Yap, the Filipino nurse who was also one of the hostages. I had mixed emotions. I tried to think clearly and suppress my emotions. But it was a futile exercise for me. Reality is reality as tragic as it may be.

"*Why do things have to end this way? These are good people. They have unjustly suffered enough for months. Why are we in this situation?*" I had to shake off my thoughts and focus on what I should do next.

I looked back to Gracia. My men were attending her. They were all concerned about her condition. Everyone was on alert and dead set on defending our position. We must ensure the safe extrication of Gracia.

After a few minutes of tactical observation, I told my troops, *"Dalhin natin sya sa taas!* [Let's bring her (Gracia) up the ridge!]" We needed a vantage point where we could secure her from any enemy counterattack while waiting for her safe evacuation to the rear and eventual medical treatment.

I called for help from our companions who were positioned at the top of the hill.

Never Give Up

Safely bringing Gracia, as well as my wounded troops, and the dead bodies of Martin and Ediborah, up the hill was no easy task. Aside from security concerns, the terrain was also challenging. Its steep slope was further complicated by its slippery condition due to the rain. Rough and tough as it was, we needed to do it. And as clear as the sunshine, the Oath of a Ranger says it all.

> "I am a Ranger. Only men with iron determination is qualified to be one. I am trained like a panther; silent, swift, fearless. My mere presence freezes the enemy's blood. I am invisible to him until the last second of his life. I rule in the mountains. I stalk in the jungle. Day or darkness, calm or storm, tireless in the hunt, fierce in the fight. I am a Ranger..."

My mind was racing – as if it was running 240mph at that point. I felt like my heart was in a Formula One race. There was no time to waste. There could be no dilly-dallying. Time was of the essence. The safety of Gracia was paramount! She deserved freedom from the sorry state she had been in for more than a year.

I stayed focused. In my head, I organized the things needed to be done fast: *"We have to secure Gracia and my wounded soldiers, gather the firearms and ammunition recovered from the terrorists, consolidate all pertinent belongings with intelligence value, arrange for medical evacuation, and lastly, bring the dead bodies of Martin, Ediborah and a few terrorists to the top of the ridge.*" Everybody was mobilized. We needed to do everything quickly as the weather might suddenly change. At that time, visibility was also limited due to rain and fog.

We struggled to bring Gracia to the top of the ridge because of the wet and slippery ground. The same was true with the dead bodies. Everyone was exhausted as we consolidated and secured the ridgeline. My troops looked unkempt with mud all over their faces and bodies. They looked horrible but I thought, *"I probably look worse right now."*

By 4:30 P.M., everyone was settled on top of the ridge. The nine wounded soldiers, Gracia, the dead bodies, and the numerous recovered items which included the chain used to tie Martin, were all in their respective places. Gracia was settled. She had been well attended to as we helped her and made her comfortable as the situation we were in would allow. Ranger Tuazon had tried to administer intravenous fluids for Gracia but wasn't able to insert the needle properly. Worse, and embarrassingly, we did not have much other than the generic pain reliever for her pain. Although I was so embarrassed, I told one of my troops to offer it to her, and she graciously accepted. Even now, I wonder whether that medication did her any good. How I wish we could have offered her something more.

"Sir, nine (9) wounded, all accounted for!", Lieutenant Andrada reported to me as he completed checking on every member of our troops. While 1Lt Andrada took care of all that was needed for safe evacuation of those needing medical attention, I also came up with an extrication plan from the area. At the same time, Team 3 under Ranger Dela Fuente secured the immediate initial MEDEVAC site and attended to the wounded Rangers.

Around that time, I was informed that troops of the 10th Scout Ranger Company and the Sniper Teams were almost in our area and were to link up with us. They were to assist in securing Gracia and preserving the encounter site. An investigation would be done by trained personnel sent by higher ups to the area soon. That was much welcome news to me. It meant more hands to help us sort things out. Most importantly, we would be able to get some rest and good chow!

Rock Steady

The 10th Scout Ranger (We Lead) Company under Cpt Albert Baloloy and the Sniper Teams led by 1Lt Lee Romero, eventually linked up with us. The Sniper Teams were composed mostly of volunteer soldiers who were undergoing the tedious Scout Sniper Course under the able tutelage of then Cpt Isagani Criste. They were all raring to fight, if still needed.

Despite the gravity of the situation, I managed to smile when I saw Cpt Baloloy. It was a huge relief to see someone you could depend on in the battlefield. Cpt Baloloy was all smiles too. I guess it was just natural for two warrior-friends to be ecstatic when they met each other on the field of battle. They laugh to their hearts' content with whatever time, or peace, they may have. After all, who knows what might happen next.

When the gun battle started, the 10SRC troops together with the Sniper Teams, quickly rushed towards our general location. They wanted to get as close as possible to us anticipating that we would be needing reinforcement to effectively contain or restrict the movement of the enemy. They knew the drill. They didn't intend to let fellow Rangers fight a war singlehandedly. Rangers always want to join fellow Rangers in a fight!

Cpt Baloloy and his troops were approximately 500 meters in map distance from our location when they heard the first volley of gunfire. Ground distance, though, was much farther. As expected, in a jungle like that of Sirawai, Zamboanga del Norte, the movement of 10SRC troops was slowed down by the up and down, rocky, slippery wet terrain. They were running and out of breath when they linked up with us. But nonetheless, they quickly buckled down to work and helped us with the clearing of the area.

Given the additional manpower of 10SRC, I was able to attend to other operational matters. The troops of Cpt Baloloy and 1Lt Romero were of great help in recovering the dead bodies of the hostages and the terrorists as well as in clearing the ridge for the landing zone. I was able to contact our Tactical Command Post and discussed our evacuation plan. According to the TCP, we should consider moving to the nearest logging road about one kilometer, map distance, from our location. Air evacuation might be an impossibility because the sky was not clear, drizzle continued, and dusk was coming soon. Moreover, the ridge was covered with small trees and light vegetation. I pondered on God's word.

> "I lift up my eyes to the mountains, where does my help come from? My help comes from the LORD, the Maker of heaven and earth." *Psalm 121:1-2 (NIV)*

I thought, "*If God made the heaven and earth, then maybe he can send the choppers despite the restricted conditions.*" I doubted it but still needed to keep my thinking sharp, because a lot of responsibility rested on me. We should make a landing zone by all means. I could barely see the logging road afar off.

"*No way can we do that. Choppers must come for Gracia and my wounded troops. No matter how many they can take in a load. My priorities are fixed. Foremost is Gracia – she must be extricated first and the soonest*", I mumbled.

I figured it would be almost impossible to traverse the challenging terrain, carry the wounded, while having the recovered enemy's belongings on top of dealing with our own heavy backpacks. Besides, it would be dark before we even reach the logging road.

Added to that was the possibility of engagement along the way with the remnants of the group we had just fought. That was definitely not a good prospect and would put everyone in danger. It was a catch-22 situation for us, so I had to think it carefully through.

I discussed with my battalion commander the proposition that medical evacuation (MEDEVAC) should be done by air. If the Philippine Air Force declined for good reasons, perhaps the Americans could offer their air assets. They might consider the idea, knowing that one of their own – Gracia, an American – was in need of crucial help. I wasn't sure whether such an action – using foreign assets for medevac purposes – would violate the VFA. I thought that maybe that particular situation might be an exception.

Amidst all the predicaments, I tried to maintain my composure. So much was at stake. My troops and Gracia depended on my good judgment. They needed to be extracted and help seemed to be hard to get right then. Why? As I was waiting for the decision of the Tactical Command Post, we initiated some measures.

"Rangers, kailangang gumawa tayo ng landing zone (LZ)! [Rangers, we need to create a landing zone (LZ)!]", I commanded, pointing towards a specific area. Every moment counted, and I decided not to waste time.

The ridge was quite small for a UH-1H (Huey) helicopter to land, but it could hover so we just needed to cut the small trees and clear the vicinity as much as we could. Everybody understood what I meant. Everyone with a bolo mobilized to clean up the designated area.

While my troops, assisted by Cpt Baloloy's Rangers, were hard at work for a LZ, my radioman handed me the radio hand set. *"Unbeatable 6 is on the line, sir"*, said my radioman.

"Unbeatable 6, Jordan 6, over!"

"Is there a landing zone?" come the voice from the other end.

"Positive, sir!" I managed a slight smile as I sensed a glimmer of hope for my request for air medevac.

"How's the sky?"

"Clear, over!"

There was indeed a LZ but barely considered a real one, and the sky was not ideally clear. But under the circumstances at that time, it was the best we could do. Yes, I made a judgment call. To me, it was better to decide and be proven wrong later than to make no decision at all. I had to say and do what was needed at that moment.

"Alright, Jordan 6. Choppers are coming. Be ready!"

Yes! Those were the words we all wanted to hear. I looked at Cpt Baloloy and the troops. I gave them the thumbs-up sign.

"Choppers are coming!" I declared. Everybody managed a sigh of relief. All our troops smiled in approval.

Everything seemed to be set, so I approached Gracia to brief her on what our next step would be. The slightly wounded Ranger Tuazon, our medic, attended to her. Ranger Eustaquio gave his *malong*, an indigenous blanket, so Gracia could keep warm. Honestly, I really did not know what to say. I was overwhelmed with everything that had transpired but I felt the need to talk to her somehow. I found it awkward. I gathered my thoughts.

"Ms. Burnham, I know you are probably angry with us," I politely said. *"I hope you understand that we were just doing our job."*

She softly but firmly responded, *"I know. We never forgot who the bad guys were and who the good guys were. I don't think of you as the bad guys."*

I felt some relief inside of me. Her words struck a positive note in my heart. I have to admit I needed that affirmation right at that moment. Never for a moment did I wish any hurt to come to people like them.

Then she asked, *"How did you find us?"*

"We've been following you all day. We saw your tracks where you crossed the logging road last night," I replied.

She told me how hungry they were after so many days without food. I could only imagine, as I recalled the remnants of the fruit they had left at the farm.

"Yeah, we saw the farm where you ate your breakfast this morning. We just kept on tracking you."

I recalled that we were so preoccupied with tracking them that we had foregone eating our own breakfast. We had a job to do and sometimes we must sacrifice. *"Even the ultimate sacrifice"*, I thought sadly.

At around 5 P.M., we got an update from the TCP that UH1H Huey helicopters, escorted by MG520s, were coming. Then after some time, we got a radio call from the lead chopper's pilot establishing contact with us.

As I listened to the chop-chop-chop sound of the rotor blades approaching, I said to myself, *"Just another day Ranger Almonares, but this one was a tough one. Thank you, Lord!"* I thought with gratefulness.

Gracia and my wounded troops were put in the lead chopper while I rode in the other chopper with the dead bodies, the recovered firearms and ammunition, and items of high intelligence value. I was tempted to keep the chain they used on Martin as remembrance of that fateful day. It was a good thing I didn't. The chains were included later with the body of evidence presented in court to convict the terrorists, ultimately leading to their imprisonment in a Philippine maximum security prison.

I was dropped off at the Joint Task Force Comet (JTF Comet) Headquarters to give a debriefing and to turn over the recovered items. Some officers chatted with me and quickly got an overview of information regarding our mission. That night, I stayed in the Task Force Headquarters mulling over everything that had transpired that day.

Seriously, I simply could not believe that so much had happened that day. I had been with my troops for just 24 hours. What a day!

Aftermath

As I lay down in my hammock that night, I could not help but think of the following day. *"I'll have lots of questions to answer soon,"* I thought, *"but for now I just need to rest."* I suddenly realized how exhausted I was, and my troops were more than dead-tired. I wondered, *"Why am I in this thing?"* Although I was both grateful and humbled to be a part of Gracia's rescue and freedom from her captors, I did not have a good idea of what God had in store for me. Only now did I figure it out.

> "You did not choose me, but I chose you and appointed you so that you might go and bear fruit - fruit that will last - and so that whatever you ask in my name the Father will give you." *John 15:16 (NIV)*

Many would later criticize us for not pursuing the enemy that fateful afternoon. Civilians and military geniuses alike thought we should have gone after the ASG immediately after the firefight subsided. A lot of news articles described the situation as some kind of failure. They likened it to what happened during the Lamitan Siege in 2001. It baffled me that people so easily gave their critical opinions on how things that Scout Rangers always do should be done. Maybe watching too many movies or playing too many computer games skews an objective perception of reality.

Reality is that combat situations are not movie scenes where the enemy is contained and static in one area, and then the hero actors quickly, neatly, and completely annihilate them all. With my unit, there were only forty of us and the four snipers under my tactical control (Tacon). Plus, I had nine wounded personnel. Under those circumstances, we needed to secure the area to ably protect our wounded troops and the rescued hostages. We also needed to secure pertinent items to be used as evidence and other enemy materiel of high value to military intelligence. Hence, logically, it was impossible for us to do a pursuit operation. I was hurt by the criticisms, but I eventually realized that it is just human nature to casually find faults instead of encouragement and constructive inputs. And perhaps, it is only someone with experience in special operations who could fully understand the situation that we were in at that time.

Reflections

Back then, I was so preoccupied with my own concerns that I was not really thinking much about God's plan for me. My schooling in the PMA and the Scout Ranger Training School (SRTS) led me to believe what William Ernest Henley wrote in his *Invictus, "I am the master of my fate: I am the captain of my soul"*. I just wanted a "progressive military career" as we call it in the academy.

God allows us opportunities in life not to satisfy our selfish ambitions but to use these platforms for His honor and glory. We can only truly achieve our goals if they are aligned with God's will and purpose. God often uses people who are not the best and the brightest so that in the end, man cannot boast but acknowledge God's sovereignty. I like what the English Standard Version of the Bible said about Gideon in *Judges 6:12,*

> "And the angel of the LORD appeared to him and said to him, "The LORD is with you, O mighty man of valor."

The truth is, Gideon was not even close to being the best. But God allowed him to lead 300 men against the large Midianite army "without even firing a single shot," as we say in modern military parlance. They simply blew their trumpets and shouted a battle cry as their burning torches and the noise simulated an attack by a large force. As a result, the Midianite army fled. This has become a symbolic military success story, just like the 300 Spartans at Thermopylae. Here is one classic example where God shows us that strength is not by "our might but by His might!" *Ephesians 6:10.*

The Road Ahead

A week after the rescue, I was informed that I was recommended for the highest medal of the land – the Medal of Valor. I personally did not believe I deserved such an award. The one who deserved the recommendation for the award, I thought, was my lead scout, Ranger Tamayo – or maybe Ranger Jagmoc, or Ranger Catague. The truth is, any of my men could have been recommended for the bravery and sacrifice they offered. Someone from the higher headquarters mentioned that if I had been wounded, I might have had a great chance to get the award. Honestly, I wasn't really hoping for it, even though it is a coveted honor. All I wanted was for my troops to be safe and for the hostages to be rescued. Of course, I don't deny that I wanted all the terrorists to get killed as well. But the world is an imperfect and fallen world where lots of things happen beyond our control.

Ranger Tamayo, together with Ranger Alexander Tolentino, died a senseless death two weeks after the rescue. They died in a vehicular accident when a military M35 truck loaded with drums of gasoline fell off of a ravine. They were riding in the truck headed to re-supply and relieve the operating troops after a 2-week respite following the rescue. Cocoy was really the epitome of a person with an indomitable spirit. After the truck fell 20 meters down the ravine seriously injuring him, he still managed to crawl the long way back atop the ridge before he expired. Truly, Cocoy was my hero. He was our unit's undisputed hero in the military mission that led to the rescue of Gracia. How I wished all the terrorists to be dead in that moment, instead of my two brave Rangers.

Yes, without hesitation, I would gladly grant the award to Ranger Tamayo. Maybe, I could have used my position as a company-grade officer to recommend him posthumously, but it wasn't ultimately my decision to be followed on the award. Lots of "what ifs" now. I will leave it at that. Like Gideon, I was not even close to being a man of valor. The troops and I were just instruments in preserving one of God's soldiers. Events happened for a reason. In God's economy, He is sovereign. I know that God has a purpose for all of us and the things that transpired did not take Him by surprise.

Invisible Wounds

Scout Rangers' battle wounds healed after many years but surely their sacrifices and heroic deeds left scars. Ranger Carlito San Pablo, for one, still has a shrapnel embedded on left side of his scalp. His wounds somehow affect his moods at times, but he beams with pride that at one point of his life he was part of a great historic event. I was not aware that before he left for that operation, he was suffering from depression because he had been bypassed twice for promotion to the next higher rank. Most of his batchmates were two ranks higher than him and it affected his confidence and morale. His wife, Jen, encouraged him that God had something in store for him. But bitterness was so evident in him as was manifested by his irritability and quick temper.

However, after the rescue of Gracia, Ranger San Pablo was promoted twice in one year because of his contribution to the accomplishment of the mission. That promotion became an instrument for him to appreciate God's greatness and goodness. He concluded that indeed God does things in His perfect time. Nowadays, he is sometimes referred to as "pastor' due to his sound spiritual advice to fellow soldiers who are in the same situation he was in before. Truly, that rescue operation impacted the lives of the Scout Rangers in many blessed ways.

Ranger San Pablo's wife was four months pregnant when she learned that he was wounded in the rescue mission. She was speechless, dumbfounded, and in tears as she knelt down on her knees while she prayed solemnly. She stormed the heavens with fervent prayers imploring the Almighty to spare her husband.

Upon learning that Carlito was confined in Camp Navarro Hospital inside the AFP Southern Command camp in Zamboanga City, Jen wished to go right away to visit him but she had no money for fare from Basilan –where their family was based at that time – to Zamboanga City. She begged the crew of the fastcraft plying the Zamboanga-Basilan sea route to allow her to board, even if there was no place to sit, because her husband was confined in the hospital due to battle wounds. According to Jen, God answered her plea and she was allowed to board the fast craft and graciously accommodated in no less than the ship captain's cabin!

The struggle of a soldier's wife is real and beyond compare. She is both the father and mother of the house while her husband is on the battlefield fighting for freedom and peace. To quote a poem written by an unknown author that best describes a military wife, let me share "Silent Ranks",

I wear no uniforms, no blues or army greens.
But I am in the military in the ranks rarely seen.
I have no rank upon my shoulders,
salutes I do not give.
But the military world is the place where I live.

I'm not in the chain of command, orders I do not get.

But my husband is the one who does,
this I cannot forget.
I'm not the one who fires the weapon,
who puts my life on the line.
But my job is just as tough.
I'm the one that's left behind.

My husband is a patriot, a brave and prideful man,
And the call to serve his country,
not all can understand.
Behind the lines I see the things needed
to keep this country free.
My husband makes the sacrifice,
but so do our kids and me.
I love the man I married. Patriotism is his life.
But I stand among the silent ranks
known as the military wife.

Every military wife plays a very important role in a soldier's life. It takes two to dance well the tango, so to speak.

Healing Time

Gracia Burnham later turned out to be one of God's remarkable evangelists, who continues to bring a lot of souls to Jesus Christ's warm embrace. She forgave the terrorists that caused harm to her and Martin. She supported the children of these terrorists. Some of those kidnappers have found freedom in Jesus Christ while inside prison.

Nowadays, Gracia is being used mightily as she tells her story all over the world. Her two books, *In the Presence of My Enemies* (2003) and *To Fly Again* (2005), are inspiring those who do not know Jesus Christ and strengthening the faith of those who follow Him.

"For it is by grace you have been saved, through faith-and this is not from yourselves, it is a gift from God-not by works, so that no one can boast." *Ephesians 2:8-9 (NIV)*

It is indeed mind-boggling how God loves the sinner and offers His forgiveness by grace through faith. I am grateful and blessed that a sinner like me can be a part of His grand plan. Truly amazing grace!

•••

At times, we may feel disqualified or unworthy to be used by God. Maybe because we've fallen short a lot of times. We forget or do not realize that His grace is enough. According to the contemporary Christian singer Matthew West, "God is in the business of using broken people and broken things." He expounded this well in a song.

"Broken Things"

If grace was a kingdom
I stopped at the gate
Thinking I don't deserve to pass through after all the
mistakes that I've made
Oh I heard a whisper
As heaven bent down
Said, "Child, don't you know that the first will be last
and the last get a crown."
Now I'm just a beggar in the presence of a King
I wish I could bring so much more
But if it's true You use broken things
Then here I am Lord, I'm all Yours
The pages of history they tell me it's true
That it's never the perfect; it's always the ones with
scars that You use

It's the rebels and the prodigals;
it's the humble and the weak
All the misfit heroes You chose
Tell me there's hope for sinners like me

Now I'm just a beggar in the presence of a King
I wish I could bring so much more
But if it's true You use broken things
Then here I am Lord, I'm all Yours
Grace is a kingdom
With gates open wide
There's a seat at the table just waiting for you
So, come on inside.

•••••

Proof of Life. The first picture of the Burnham couple that came out publicly to prove they were still alive. This picture was accompanied by a video of the terrorists to relay their demands (November 2001)

Deep in the Jungles. Taken during one of our operations to locate and rescue the hostages (2001)

"Mandirigma" is a Tagalog word for warriors, the 15th Scout Ranger Company name. These Scout Rangers lived up to their name and the First Scout Ranger Regiment's expectations.

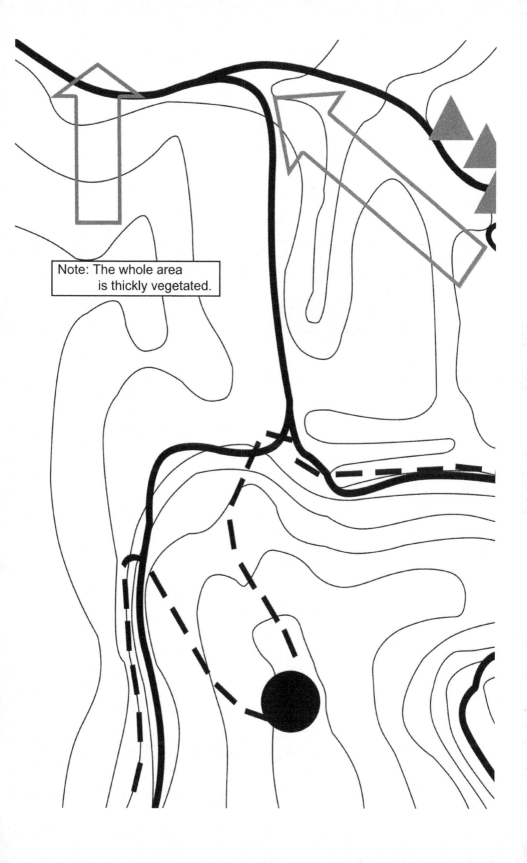

Note: The whole area is thickly vegetated.

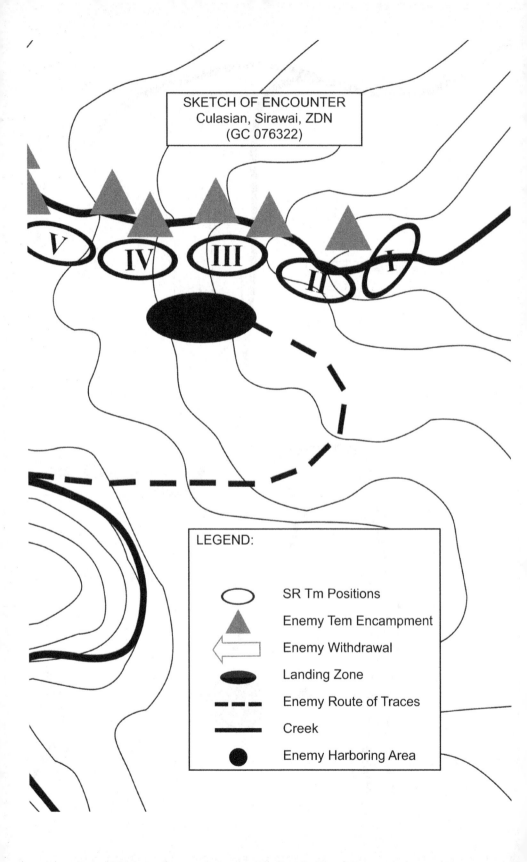

Back Home. Gracia was grateful to God and joyful to see the rest of her family.

First Reunion. Meeting Gracia at Tyndale House Publishers in Carol Stream, IL (2003)

Internationally Sought-After Speaker. Gracia Burnham made global impact as she travels to tell her story. Her books "In the Presence of My Enemies" (2003) and "To Fly Again" (2005) are both best sellers.

CHAPTER 7

FLEETING GLORY

"All people are like grass,
and all their glory is like the flowers of the field;
the grass withers and the flowers fall,
but the word of the Lord endures forever."

— Peter 1:24-25 (NIV)

The day after the rescue, I was brought back to our camp in Basilan by the UH1H helicopter. Again, I was the only passenger. The first person who met me as I dismounted from the chopper was the commander of the U.S. Special Forces, an Army Captain and also a member of U.S. Military Academy Class of 1995. He hugged and congratulated me like a brother who had just received his championship trophy after a grueling competition. He knew well how rough the operation had been and that to survive unscathed wasn't a given.

The U.S. Special Forces Captain told me, *"That was so brave of you to crawl and get close within 10-15 meters on the enemy. Oh man, that's too dangerous! I really doubt whether we could do such a thing. Lead the way, brother!"* I was surprised and elated as he expressed his admiration for what we had done, despite the casualties.

I couldn't help but be emotional when that U.S. Special Forces officer expressed his gratitude to me and my troops. No matter how simple and informal it was, his gesture was a rare and precious occasion in my life. I cherished the compliment from one warrior to another – it's an honor.

Whether he was only trying to be nice or humble, it really made me teary-eyed. I thought, *"Look at this American Special Forces guy. He appreciated what we did while some of my own countrymen are so eager to point their fingers at mistakes they thought we committed."*

As I was approaching my barracks, I could see media people. I recognized some local and national media personalities, but I couldn't recall their names anymore. They asked me if they could have a live interview with me. I politely told them that I was not in a position to give details at the moment, that I needed clearance from the Department of National Defense (DND). In the first place, officers of my rank never accommodated media interviews. We let spokesmen handle media relations. To me, they appeared frustrated when they couldn't get anything from me. I would have loved to help them do their jobs, but there were set official procedures to follow. I understood their frustrations. Merely going to our camp was not easy. In fact, it was very dangerous. They expected to at least have something for coverage, something to report to their respective bosses at the end of the day. They were just doing their jobs. They went their way home with nothing from me. I felt for them.

Unfamiliar Terrain

In my limited understanding, I thought the rescue of Gracia and the death of her captors would end the whole thing and would allow us some respite. But that was not the case for me. There were a lot of things that followed, like the Senate inquiry as to why Martin and Ediborah died during the rescue. For whatever reasons they thought they needed an inquiry.

It did not really sound good to me. What else could I say? Everything was, or would be, in the After Battle Report (ABR) duly signed and vetted by my superior officers. I was just an operator – a Scout Ranger destined and trained for fighting in the jungle. The august halls of the Senate or any other esteemed bodies did not need my presence. I would rather go on combat operations for days on end in hostile territories, rather than be in an air-conditioned room in full Army regalia answering questions that my superiors could explain way better than I could. I thought, *"The Army paid me, as a Lieutenant, to do rough stuff in the field not in some fancy halls. I could give more value to their (Army) money's worth out there in the jungle."*

Fortunately, some knowledgeable people stepped in and gave their opinion of the incident. One of them was retired MGen Ramon Farolan, a member of PMA Class of 1956, who wrote in his *Philippine Star* column about the "concept of arm-chair generals." We do not personally know each other, but I address him as Cavalier or "Cav", as fellow PMA graduates address each other. I was not able to thank him personally but I was so grateful for his firm stand defending our soldiers who were on actual battlegrounds.

The inquiry never happened. In my mind, it would not have brought anything good anyway.

That night, after my encounter with the U.S. Special Forces officer, I was informed that I needed to report to the DND and personally brief the Secretary of Defense, the late General Angelo Reyes. The good Secretary and I talked over the phone and he gave me specific orders. He needed some information because he would soon be interviewed by *ABS-CBN's* Ms. Korina Sanchez, a well-known media personality in the Philippines.

When I got to Headquarters DND in Camp Aguinaldo, I did not know that the DND staff had invited the *Philippine Daily Inquirer*, a print media organization in the Philippines, to interview me on the rescue operation. That took me by surprise. As much as I wasn't comfortable about the interview, I nonetheless complied. They eventually published the story. After that day, other media interviews were also set up and I politely obliged. My days in

Manila went by with me doing media engagements. On the side though, I also did other duties for my unit. After fully complying with all my scheduled official commitments, I went back to Basilan and continued with my Scout Ranger life.

Unexpected Respite

On one fine day, Captain Dick Ebo, a PMA classmate, told me to prepare for a possible trip to the United States. He said, *"The Commanding General of the Philippine Army, Lieutenant General Dionisio Santiago, invites you to join his party that will visit the US Army War College."* LtGen Santiago was to be the Guest of Honor and Speaker at an event in that institution where they would honor him as one of its outstanding alumni. I was in the hinterlands of Basilan when I received the call to report to Manila in preparation for the US trip.

To be invited is an honor, but to actually join the official party of the Philippine Army's commanding general is both an honor and privilege. Up until now, I don't know whether I deserved to have both. But just the same, as an obedient soldier, I reported to Manila.

While I was in the US, I was able to call Gracia Burnham. It was our first conversation after she left the Philippines for the US. I was not able to get updates about her because I was so busy doing my "Scout Ranger" activities in the jungles of Sulu and Basilan. I was back to the routine things that we do as soldiers, and as Scout Rangers – we are better off in the jungle.

Realizing the publicity Gracia's story generated and how she used it to spread positivity and the word of God, I was so amazed about how things worked for her. I felt so blessed to be part of her story. I never realized her global impact and most of all how God was mightily showing her the way. She got a lot of attention through the international media. I was so happy for her – then and now.

My U.S. sojourn allowed me also to visit my brother Jessie, who is a nurse in Illinois. He is a pillar of our family, the one that everyone can depend on at any time.

While the United States of America is a beautiful place, I felt it was not the country for me. I told myself, *"This place is not for me"*. I longed to go back to Basilan and be with my troops. I really missed my rugged band of Scout Rangers.

Though it was a nice trip, I hardly felt the urge to visit the U.S. again. My heart yearned much for the Philippines and to serve her until I die. Truly, I had no idea what God would do with me in the years to come. Figuratively, I was like a water hyacinth in the river of life – I go wherever the water current takes me.

Home with my Buddies

Back in the Philippines, I continued with my duties as the commander of the 15th Scout Ranger (*Mandirigma*) Company.

It was very rewarding for my men to be promoted to the next higher rank by virtue of their awards and firearms recovered. They were elated as their promotions meant additional compensation for them, which in turn, benefitted their families. Soldiers readily go to battle and do risky missions, not because they hate their adversaries but because they love more what they left behind at their homes and their communities. To reward them with promotions and additional compensation was probably the best recognition they could get from the government for their hard work. Being their commander and seeing them so happy brought tears to my eyes – it still does. Yes, those were the glorious days of the 15th Scout Ranger (*Mandirigma*) Company.

In March 2003, while operating in the mountains of Jolo, I was informed that I would be awarded on Philippine Army Day with the Distinguished Conduct Star, the second highest combat award in the AFP, by then President Gloria Macapagal-Arroyo. I was one of the awardees during the Philippine Army Day. I got a lot of attention and did media interviews after the ceremony.

When I went home to Iloilo, the local media also requested an interview. I wasn't media savvy but I learned to answer in a "politically-correct" manner. I would always say, *"I was just in a situation where I needed to do something. Any officer, or soldier, in my position will always do his best for the accomplishment of the mission."* From what I had read in books and heard on television, the media world could be tricky. It could make or break me. If I got careless, the unintended consequences were cruel. I was learning.

Friends and people I knew would congratulate me for "the feat" and I would modestly acknowledge their compliments. I would usually downplay my role in the rescue, but in reality I was struggling to be humble. There was so much pride deep in my heart. The wrong kind of confidence was building up in my heart. I was humble outside but full of haughtiness inside. Funny and ignorant I was.

I failed to see the real purpose of why I had been placed by God in that position. I believed that what we accomplished was solely because of our sheer courage and superb combat skills. That was very far from the truth. Actually, I was being audaciously stupid and proud.

The Foray

On July 27, 2003, the Oakwood Mutiny happened. The name was derived from the name of the Oakwood Premier Ayala Center (it has a new name now), located at the heart of Makati City, which was occupied by more than 300 soldiers from different elite units of the AFP to air their grievances against the alleged corruption in the administration of then President Gloria Macapagal-Arroyo.

I got involved in this operation as it was mostly composed of our classmates from PMA and colleagues in the military service. I do not and would not want to discuss the merits or demerits of that incident anymore. It probably served its purpose in our history. As for me, I did not join those who went to the Oakwood Hotel because of my own convictions (which prevailed over my emotions). I did not have any negative feelings towards those who joined, or towards those who did not. I realized I couldn't handle the intricacies and complexities of politics. I am a simpleton in the world of politics.

Events that led up to and followed Oakwood made me ask a lot of questions on our country's socio-political and economic issues. Those topics seemed strange and confusing to an infantryman like me. Questions led to more questions and there didn't seem to be concrete answers for the problems facing our well-loved Philippine society. It was as if the malaises afflicting Philippine society were individually dissected and given serious scrutiny – only that the ones analyzing them were not medical doctors or even scientists, but a group of battle-scarred soldiers.

Steadily, our small group discussions further opened my mind. Soon, there was no stopping my craving for a better understanding of things that seemed so alien to me for many years. Who would? For the longest time, I had been so focused on battling armed elements nationwide. I began to realize that military operations had become my world – war had become my life. It consumed me.

Through more discourse and reading, my socio-political consciousness was awakened. It made me humbly realize that I was a Scout Ranger trained to fight bloody battles. I was willing to fight in actual combat, but I did not have the ability to fight other challenges outside of that. The boondocks were my comfort zone and I understood that the political arena was not my battlefield.

My thoughts about my interrupted foray into the realm of politics is this: *"Appropriate political understanding and wisdom is necessary for every military officer or any person charged with leading an organization, whether in private capacity or in public service. He must be educated and experienced enough to manage complexities, and rightly decide under extreme situations for his organization. However, overconfidence or even under self-estimation of one's ability impacts the subject institution. Imprudent decisions or ill-timed actions usually bring negative effects both to the individual and to the institution that person represents. Preparation, assessment, planning, training and execution is paramount in everything we do. Knowing myself, I focused to what I can fairly comprehend and accomplish based on my skills set at that time. I could not in conscience go beyond what I cannot deliver as planned, or much more, as promised."*

New Hope with New Plans

In September 2003, my family and I went to the United States of America (U.S.A.) with new plans. We wanted to start, by God's grace, our life anew. We had good intentions and an honest-to-goodness plan of finding a new beginning in America. But that would not be the case. We realized we were not prepared for that giant leap – from Philippine life to American life. We needed to rethink our original plan.

Yes, it was hard for us because we had a visitor's visa. I went through a lot of difficulties, especially emotionally. The U.S. is a great place to get a fresh start in life. But as I contemplated our chances as a family in the U.S., I was ushered into the reality of US life where loads of patience, humility, hard work and perseverance – including reinventing myself in many forms – are keys to success. I felt intimidated inside. It seemed I could not hack it well in the U.S. It appeared we had no spot to start our life anew even in the vastness of America. I had bouts of depression, and I felt I was steadily moving towards rock bottom inside. Self-pity was killing me, compounded by the thought that I was a respected soldier-warrior back home. Maybe I was just so intimidated by the way of life in the U.S. and its fast-paced tempo each day. Or perhaps, I was just stubbornly proud for nothing – so full of myself.

God allowed me to face those challenges to mold me into the

person He wants me to be. I was humbled. He was getting my attention this time. Our initial U.S. experience was difficult financially, emotionally and psychologically for my family. I needed to focus and effectively lead as a father and husband because my family's well-being was at stake.

Momentous Meeting

On December 12, 2003, Gracia and I met at Tyndale House Publishers in Carol Stream, Illinois. It was awkward but also a healing moment for me to talk to her personally.

She wrote, in her book "To Fly Again" (2005), *"When I stood up to shake his hand and say good-bye, I realized once again that forgiveness is a choice. Had his bullet possibly struck my husband? There is no way to know, and what good would it serve to know? Far better to forgive and move on."* There seemed to be a kind of anger in her but I did somehow understand. It is her choice to be mad, or to forgive us.

We will never fully understand the pain she experienced unless we were in her situation. Gracia had every right to express what she felt and wanted to say. War and violence changes a lot of people, especially those who are directly involved in it. War, whatever we conceive it to be, indisputably leaves a deep scar in our soul. To us soldiers, there is always a part of us that was left on the battlefield. Many can't understand; but whatever that is, it will always be sacred to us.

It still breaks my heart to remember that those who fought with me, and died left widows and orphans. It is hard to think about it, but it is real.

> "And as it is appointed unto men once to die, but after this the judgment." *Hebrews 9:27 (KJV)*

We will all eventually die and the manner in which it happens is beyond our control. We are all dependent on God's grace and mercy.

I didn't choose to be on that rescue team. In fact, I was ordered to go there the day before it happened, even though I was hurting and hampered by the blisters on my feet. However, there were orders to follow. It was my judgment call to firmly insist that we follow the tracks as I talked with my Battalion Commander that day. That decision led to consequences, but I believe God put me in that situation. I take responsibility for any flaws and imperfections in that operation. All I know is that we did our very best and we put our lives at stake. What good does it serve for me to wonder if the bullet which hit Martin came from us? Nothing positive, I think. There is no need for us to punish ourselves unnecessarily, no need to self-flagellate.

So I moved on and vowed to do better for myself, my family, my fellowmen, and most of all, for Him.

•••••

Debriefing the Secretary. With the late Secretary Angelo Reyes of the Department of National Defense after my debrief on the rescue mission (June 2002).

Visit to the US Army War College. (L-R) Lt Gen Dionisio Santiago, myself, US Army Ranger General, and Cpt Roy Derilo (October 2002)

The Aide-de-Camp. Cpt Dexter Ebo, aide-de-camp of Lt Gen Dionisio Santiago and my PMA classmate, and myself. (October 2002)

Best Enlisted Personnel. Ranger Radney Magbanua (left) and Ranger Cirilo Jagmoc (right) flanking me. Photo taken after they were awarded as the FSRR's Best Enlisted Personnel of the year. (November 2002)

Duly Awarded. Philippine President Gloria Macapagal-Arroyo awarding me the Distinguished Conduct Star – the AFP's second highest combat award – during the Philippine Army Day celebration in Fort Andres Bonifacio, Metro Manila. (March 2003)

CHAPTER **8**

IN HIS TIME

*"The LORD is good to those whose hope is in him,
to the one who seeks him."*

— *Lamentations 3:25 (NIV)*

After we returned to the Philippines from the United States in 2004, my wife and I had a plan. We would go back to school to take up Nursing. After we graduated and passed all the required examinations, we would immigrate to the United States and the nursing profession would be our means.

It was not a simple plan. It would entail a lot of hard work and time. It was a long shot but we were determined and desperate to make the most of whatever opportunity was available to us.

My brother Jessie, who is a nurse in an American hospital, would support us financially in the meanwhile. He was God's emissary to us. *Nonoy* Jessie understood well that we would need a stable income to sustain our plan.

By God's grace, we became full-time students and took our Bachelor of Science in Nursing in Bacolod, a city in Negros Island far from our home in Iloilo. Our daughter, Bea, was only 5 years old. We were only able to see her every two weeks because we couldn't afford to go home every week. We needed to scrimp and save on our minimal resources. After all, we were only living on the generosity and support of our families, particularly that of *Nonoy* Jessie.

My older brother, Jessie, was the instrument God used for us to be where we are right now. He is not a perfect man, but for me, he had been used by God to show us a perfect example of grace and mercy. He had been a Registered Nurse in the State of Illinois for 25 years. He helped our whole clan financially by sending our nephews and nieces to school. He even supported less-privileged children unrelated to us by paying for their formal education.

He takes charge of the needs of the whole family. *Nonoy* Jessie paid off my loans from the Armed Forces when I bowed out of the service. He even paid my financial loans in Canada years later. The list goes on. I can't count all the good things he has done for all of us. But more importantly, he redeemed me in the truest sense of the word.

Back to School

Our plan to study Nursing had financial, emotional, and psychological consequences. It tested our mettle as a family and as individuals. We were essentially starting from scratch in school, and most of our classmates were in their teens and early twenties. We had to learn and relearn a lot of things to fit in. Fortunately, our classmates were gracious and kind enough to assist us as we adapted to our 'new environment'. Three years of school seemed like ten years. I don't know how we endured it.

After we both passed the Nursing Licensure Examination in the Philippines (NLE-Philippines), National Council Licensure Examination-RN (NCLEX-US), and Test of English as a Foreign Language (TOEFL), we thought all would be smooth for our migration to the U.S. That was far from reality. What came next was a long and very challenging journey.

Most of the time, we think we make our own plans and timetable.

We trust our intelligence, talents, skills and resources. It seems like we are in control of our lives. After everything we have gone through, I can now easily relate to what the Apostle James said,

> "Now listen, you who say, 'Today or tomorrow we will go to this or that city, spend a year there, carry on business and make money.' Why, you do not even know what will happen tomorrow. What is your life? You are a mist that appears for a little while and then vanishes."
> *James 4:13-14 (NIV)*

Likewise, *Proverbs 19:21 (ESV)* clearly stated also,

> "Many are the plans in the mind of a man, but it is the purpose of the Lord that will stand."

Our plan to immigrate was delayed due to visa retrogression for nurses. We waited for quite some time, and it was frustrating. It seemed that everything we had worked hard for years was in jeopardy. Visa retrogression seemed remote and unusual but it was possible.

At that time, an article in the *South Florida Sun Sentinel*, immigration attorney Daniel Sibirsky discussed the fact that the U.S. State Department had enacted "retrogression" for Registered Nurse and Physical Therapist Immigrant Visas (green cards). Sibirsky explained: *"Visa 'retrogression' occurs when immigrant visas are not immediately available and a backlog, meaning a very long line, is created for green cards because the number of applicants in a given year is greater than the number of visas available."*

As it turned out, the U.S. Congress established an annual quota for the number of green cards that can be issued each fiscal year. Registered nurses were part of the EB-3 visa category, along with other general professional occupations such as engineers, accountants, and the like.

Sibirsky pointed out that *"the EB-3 visa category is experiencing a backlog of five years, which means that a hospital currently sponsoring a completely qualified foreign nurse in 2007 to fill the vacancy of registered nurses will have to wait until 2012 for a visa to become available for that nurse."*

Sibirsky argued that nurses, especially, should have been exempted from the retrogression because the U.S. was still suffering from the lack of nurses. Alas, the nurses could do nothing else but bide their time.

This period was both tough and very humbling for my wife and me. We had a child to provide for and had no stable income to sustain our needs as a family. My brother Jessie – God bless his heart – continued to support us wholeheartedly.

Not wanting to dwell too much on temporary setbacks, we decided to work as volunteer nurses in local hospitals. It was a good decision. We not only earned more medical experience, but we also gained new friends. Volunteer work made our time worthwhile.

Spiritual Milestone

In 2007, as we contemplated our plans, our hearts rejoiced to see what God had done in our lives. As we recalled what we had gone through and how we had survived all those challenging years, we knew that God was so faithful to us.

I began to read the Bible on a deeper level. God opened my heart and mind through the guidance of the Holy Spirit to understand my purpose. I had so much desire and hunger for His Word. Often in my solitude, I would become emotional as I remembered the years I had squandered His blessings and lived outside His will. This passage of the Scripture brings tears to my eyes,

"Don't let the excitement of youth cause you to forget your Creator. Honor him in your youth before you grow old and say, "Life is not pleasant anymore." *Ecclesiastes 12:1 (NLT)*

Feeling energized by my new-found zest for spiritual pursuit, I started to attend church services regularly. For years, I had been remiss in my obligation to Him. Sadly, my failure was all due to excessive self-aggrandizement. I prayed so hard and often found myself crying to God, asking for mercy and salvation for my wife and daughter. Blessed as we were, my wife and daughter both thrived in their spiritual growth in the knowledge and grace of the Lord Jesus Christ. I knew then, as I know now, that God answered my fervent prayers, and He would make me the happiest man on earth one day.

Blessed to Serve

In 2008, our family – the Almonares clan – was blessed to have an opportunity to start a small church. Initially, we hosted church services in our old ancestral home. It was an honor to be given the opportunity to contribute positively to the church ministry, and we were grateful as a family.

On Thanksgiving Day in November of 2008, our pastor announced to the congregation that there was a good soul willing to finance the construction of a new building. He said, *"We only needed a parcel of land to build it."* No one from among us expected such good news.

Everybody was jubilant at seeing God's goodness and provision. To my surprise, I learned later that the "good soul" mentioned by our pastor was my brother Jessie! I was speechless. I was overwhelmed by my brother's generosity.

When I regained my composure, I raised my hand and walked towards our pastor. I whispered to him, *"We already have a vacant lot for the new building."* He looked at me puzzled. I simply smiled back at him. After church services, I approached him and explained what I meant.

My parents gave parcels of land to each of us siblings to build our homes if we so desired. When I learned the need for a parcel of land for the new church, I decided to reciprocate, on behalf of the congregation, my brother's generosity. Hence, I gave up my parcel of land from my parents to be used for the new building.

We were already blessed. We had a small house from a government loan when my wife and I were still in government service. My philosophy is simple: *"In this life, we only need one home, and that parcel of land was not mine. It was only given to me by my parents. Everything comes from God, and they all must be rightfully offered back to Him." Philippians 3:20 (NLT)* says,

> "But we are citizens of heaven, where the Lord Jesus Christ lives. And we are eagerly waiting for Him to return as our savior."

Earthly homes are temporal but God's home is eternal.

My wife and I started to get involved in church ministry. My sisters Helen, Vinia, and Linnea became officers of our church. They were so committed to sustain what had been started. Eventually, our brothers Rey, Roy, and Ednathan also helped financially in the completion of the building.

The generosity started by our brother Jessie sparked volunteerism in our community, especially amongst our family members. And soon the rest of our clan offered, not only their resources, but also their time and technical expertise. The work became more fun and easier for everyone. It was a joy to be part of the ministry. Everybody "offered themselves as a living sacrifice", says *Romans 12:1.*

Even now, God continues to work in the lives of people who make up Highlight Fundamental Baptist Church. Serving in the ministry is truly the experience of a lifetime, beyond human understanding. We always feel blessed!

Humbling

Sometime in August 2009, our pastor gave me an opportunity to be the worship leader. I was surprised. I knew it was a serious responsibility. But our pastor's wisdom was beyond me. I needed to step up, but not of my own strength. *Philippians 4:13 (NKJV)* aptly says, "I can do all things through Christ who strengthens me."

To rectify my inadequacy in the knowledge of Scriptures, I enrolled in a Bible correspondence course. It was a challenge for me, but I was very willing to learn. God was calling me to serve Him – I needed to be up to His minimal standard at the very least. My efforts paid off and my church congregation recognized and trusted my ability. Guess what? They allowed me to teach Sunday School for adults! The assignment was a big leap for me in our ministry – which I, myself, could not believe!

Can you imagine? From using M-16 rifle, I'm now clinging to *John 3:16!* From appreciation of the power of M-14 rifle, I am now in awe of *John 14*. The responsibility, as well as the recognition, given to me by our church elders truly inspired me.

But as many would say, blessings and surprises come in bundles, which not only made me elated but grateful as well.

Ena, my wife, joined the church choir and other women's ministry. Her move surprised and made me happy because I knew she was not an extrovert who could easily mingle even in a small group. Her joining the choir and other church activities were a sudden turn-around. She came out of her shell and began openly working for Him while supporting my efforts too.

As I steadily gained confidence in Christ, and also earned the trust of fellow church members, other churches invited me to share my testimony. I was used as an instrument to encourage other believers, as well as guide unbelievers to the saving knowledge of the Lord Jesus Christ. Everything appeared to be moving forward for me. I could not easily believe that a few months back I was so reluctant to participate in church ministry. It was as if black had turned to white in an instant!

Bible and Basketball

Sometime in December 2009, I organized a Basketball ministry for 13 year olds and under. I introduced a different approach to training: Bible-and-Basketball in one. Many were surprised and wondered how would we do it. Isn't basketball supposed to be about shooting, dribbling, teamwork, and winning?

Before we started our drills and games, I made it a point that we take to heart the basics of the gospel. I began to make the sport not only about physical skills development but a spiritual enhancement program, too. Many of them found my approach unusual but came to embrace it as we went along every training day. The following were some of the basics I taught:

First, we are all sinners.

> "For all have sinned and fall short of the glory of God."
> *Romans 3:23 (NIV)*

Second, we are not reconciled with God because of sin, but there is a solution.

> "For the wages of sin is death but the gift of God is eternal life in Christ Jesus our Lord." *Romans 6:23 (NIV)*

Lastly, God loves us so much that He gave us his only son as a sacrifice for that sin.

> "For God so loved the world that He gave His one and only Son, that whoever believes in Him shall not perish but have eternal life." *John 3:16 (NIV)*

I continued to introduce my team to the saving knowledge of the

Lord Jesus Christ for many months. Some of them had no fathers or mothers to look up to. They were only interested in learning basketball each Saturday, but God was using our program as a platform to reveal Himself to those kids. God's grace, after all, offers a fresh start.

When summer basketball league in our town rolled around, we decided to join the competition. We participated in the 13-and-under category. I started to train them at a higher level. They were upbeat and always excited to experience new basketball lessons.

After many months of making the kids learn the basics of basketball, I introduced them to the concept of winning not only in basketball, but more importantly, in life. They understood that basketball was only a part of their life, never their whole life. The sport was a means to develop the positive character needed to succeed in life. To emphasize, we made *"Winners in life never quit"* as our motto, explained further that *"Winners never quit and quitters never win"*. Our 'battle cry' was,

> "With God all things are possible"
> *Matthew 19:26 (NKJV)*

We called our ball club the Pathfinder's Ball Club. Our theme verse was, *John 14:6 (NKJV)* which says,

"I am the way, the truth, and the life. No one comes to the Father except through Me."

I trained them like Scout Rangers – focused and unrelenting. I shared with them one of the Scout Rangers' favorite mantras to resolve anything and everything, *"Surrender is not a Ranger word!"*

Human resiliency with faith in God are the two best combinations one can have to tackle the challenges in life. They would get fired up every time I would tell them that. The kids were so into the program that they asked for more activities aside from the regular basketball drills. We even had road runs with Scout Ranger chants and attitude.

"We are Rangers! Mighty, mighty Rangers! Wherever we go! People want to know who we are! Haha! Hehe! Hoho!"

It was really fun.

Every time we did road runs, people were all smiles as the "little Scout Rangers" passed by them. Many were amazed at the transformation they were seeing. Villagers saw how the kids were developing from being pesky, to being prim and focused on positive goals. But little did the people know the high level of determination the kids had to put in to succeed, not only in basketball but in life. They felt empowered by their new skills and never-say-die attitude to excel.

As the training progressed, the kids steadily developed mental toughness and physical endurance. Each day, they were excited to test their new-found knowledge and skills. Our whole family and the church supported us in many ways. The modest basketball training program that started as a surprise to many, suddenly became the focus of everybody's attention. I myself was utterly amazed by the support we started getting.

From Zeroes to Heroes

Basketball is supposed to be a "game of heights", and our team was deficient in that area compared to other teams. Whether we liked it or not, we had to fight it out. We needed to find ways to even out the handicap, or at least compensate a bit for what we lacked. But while physically our team was not gifted 'vertically', we decided to focus more on attitude, and on that special something that is invisible to the eye but matters most – our indomitable spirit. That is where we would hit them the most, and by the grace of God, nobody would equal us on that area of the competition. Yes, steady and sure, we were determined to win one day at a time!

When we were first presented in the tournament, everyone's eyes were on us. They appeared surprised and wondered how our small line-up would fare in the world of physical giants. But the thing was, many had no idea what was in our heart.

Early in the tournament, we established a reputation of being a team of "midget-giants" – physically small but with extremely huge heart. We won our games one at a time. We clawed our way up the ladder of the rankings steadily. Eventually, we got to the championship. Early in the final game, we were initially overpowered but never outfought. We fought harder and won! We were no longer the "midget-giants" but the tournament champions!

Yes, it was just plain basketball. But in the eyes of the kids, the experience, the honor of winning the championship, and the recognition were everything to them. To most of the team members, it was their first time to be publicly recognized, and have something to be proud of. But I was the proudest. Not because I got the Best Coach Award, and my nephew Jared got the Most Valuable Player (MVP) Award, but because I saw how those kids earned their rightful place in the hearts of our town. They became instant heroes and all the kids wanted to be like them.

Indeed, God uses circumstances to reveal himself. We could have lost the tournament and still believed in His promises, but what a fitting moment to be victorious. It was so rewarding for all of us. The once "inferior kids" turned out to be confident but humble, always acknowledging that whatever they had and have now, came from God.

A Memorable Experience

In June 2010, through the effort and appropriate coordination of Major Ronald Bautista, one of my classmates in the PMA, we were invited to visit Camp General Macario Peralta in Jamindan, Capiz. Camp Peralta is the headquarters of the 3rd Infantry (Spearhead) Division of the Philippine Army and was at that time under the leadership of MGen Vicente Porto, a member of PMA "*Makatarungan*" Class of 1978. Major John Andrada, my former Ex-O in the 15SRC who at that time was assigned with the 3rd Civil Military Operations Battalion, also helped in facilitating our camp visit.

Cpt Bautista made it possible for us to visit and even stay inside the camp. It was a treat for the kids to celebrate their victory, but it was also a chance to introduce them to soldiery so they could get a realistic glimpse of the regimented life, as well as the values and ethos the soldiers live by. We all wanted the kids to keep the spirit of winning alive in them. Imagine, in a few months of dedication and hard work, they had gone from being "zero to heroes".

When I told the kids about the invitation, they were excited though they had no full knowledge of what they could do inside one of the biggest AFP camps. Kids being kids, they were just glad to be invited and visit a new place. To a majority of the team, it was their first time to be outside our province, or to visit the province of Capiz.

At Camp Peralta, the kids were briefed on what soldiers do for them and for the entire country. The enthusiastic kids had all sorts of questions which the officer in-charge clearly answered. After the briefing, we were ushered to witness a combat show by the Infantry, Artillery, and Armor Units. The kids were in awe. It was a show they'd never witnessed before in their young lives. Afterwards, they toured within the camp while mingling with other soldiers who acted as both their tour guides and big brothers. The experience was truly remarkable not only for the kids but also for the adults accompanying the team. Simply put, the gracious invitation was an unforgettable experience for all of us. *Hooaah!*

I do not know the exact impact of that ministry on the lives of those kids back then or even now. Only God knows, and I trust His ways. All I know is that those experiences had a great impact on my family's spiritual growth. It was preparation for us in the battles to come.

Family is Love

Looking back at our family's experience with training those kids in my hometown, I can't help but reminisce and reflect on my days at the PMA faraway from my beloved Iloilo. The rigidity of cadet life made many cadets, including me, long for the comforts of our respective families, of our homes, and of our communities. Our stay in the Academy not only challenged us but also made us realize the inviolable value of having a family that we could depend on at any time.

The PMA, while training us to become good military officers, also developed us into exemplary family men. They provided us with a "home away from home" called the Foster Parents Program in our third year. Foster parents volunteered to provide us with parental guidance and a place to stay in Baguio during our "privileges." A part of the "privileges' was to go out of the camp during our free time, as long as we had no academic deficiencies. The academy scheduled a "Family Day," a whole day of bonding and fellowship with other cadets and their respective foster parents, brothers, and sisters.

My foster parents were Tom and Amy Morado. Daddy Tom as we called him is a retired U.S Navy serviceman. They decided to settle in Baguio after he retired on August 31, 1989, leaving their three grown up children in the United States. One time, they went to PMA to watch the parade and review of the cadets. They were so impressed. Then they heard that the Academy was looking for foster parents to join the program. They signed up.

We were given a questionnaire about our food preferences. Without any inkling as to its consequences, I honestly indicated that my favorite was "dried fish". Now, my foster parents were American citizens and spent much of their lives living in the U.S. They had a very nice house in Baguio with all kinds of furnishings that I never experienced in my life. Yet, they chose me despite that food preference. Mommy Amy cooked fried dried fish for me every time I visited them, despite its undesirable odor that stuck to their curtains and every corner of their beautiful home. Every simple gesture they did for me made me feel loved. They visited us at times at the Academy if we were unable to visit them due to our hectic schedule.

Admittedly, I am not good with words, but I can truthfully tell the whole world that I am so grateful and blessed to have had the foster parents who took care of me during those years. The PMA's Foster Parents program was indeed a transformative experience for me. To this day, it is amazing that we still keep in touch. God has truly placed people in our lives to be a part of us and be instruments of His love.

Thank you, Dad Tom, Mom Amy and the rest of your family. You blessed me in many ways!

•••••

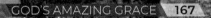

Classmates Forever. Ena and I were classmates during our university days (1987-1991), and we were classmates again when we enrolled in Nursing School at Riverside College, Bacolod City. (2004-2007)

Bachelor of Science in Nursing, Section Tango, Riverside College. (March 2007)

JOHN 14:6
36
DETERMINATION

MATTHEW 5:16
33
DISCIPLINE

Bible Basketball Uniforms

To God Be the Glory. Giving thanks to God after winning the Alimodian Summer League 13 and Under Championship. (May 2010)

Basketball Clinic. Teaching the kids of the soldiers of the 3rd Infantry Division the basics of basketball. (June 2010)

(L-R) Major Inocencio, myself, and Major John Andrada, my former Executive Officer in 15SRC.

With my PMA classmate Ronald Bautista. He was responsible for our invitation to visit the camp of the 3rd Infantry (Spearhead) Division at Jamindan, Capiz. (June 2010)

(L-R) Myself, Dad Tom, my classmate and foster brother, George Bergonia, and Mom Amy (ca. 1994)

Family Day. (Top L-R) Cdt Antonio Salgado, Cdt Alvin Hate, Cdt Arturo Veloso, Cdt Gerald Narvasa, and Cdt Rommel Conte ('96). (Bottom L-R) Dad Tom, Mom Amy, George Bergonia, Sandy David, and myself.

CHAPTER 9

NEW HOME

"The steadfast love of the LORD never ceases; his mercies never come to an end; they are new every morning; great is your faithfulnes."

— Lamentations 3:22-23 (ESV)

In November 2010, we had an opportunity to immigrate to Toronto, Canada under the skilled category as nurses. It gave us a ray of hope. But at the same time, it was hard for us to leave because of everything that had happened and was still happening in the church ministry. It was an emotional moment for all of us. But God had his own plans. And surely, it would come to pass regardless.

Toronto, the capital of the province of Ontario, is a major Canadian city along Lake Ontario's northwestern shore. Toronto is the largest city in Canada by population, with 2,731,571 residents in 2016. It's a dynamic metropolis with a downtown of soaring skyscrapers, all dwarfed by the iconic, free standing CN Tower. The city has many green spaces, from the orderly oval of Queens Park to the 400-acre High Park with its trails, sports facilities and zoo. The city is a breathtaking place to visit, and to reside.

Toronto is an international center for business and finance. Generally considered the financial capital of Canada, Toronto has a high concentration of banks and brokerage firms on Bay

Street, in the Financial District. Toronto, aside from being a diverse city, is truly beautiful.

Our apartment was strategically located along Yonge Street, a major arterial route connecting the shores of Lake Ontario in Toronto to Lake Simcoe, a gateway to the Upper Great Lakes. The subway station was just 50 meters from our apartment. Our first apartment, where we stayed for a year, had been a 15-minute bus ride from the subway. We would have to wait 15-20 minutes at the bus stop in order to connect to the nearest subway station. It was very challenging to be waiting for the bus during the winter season with temperatures of -10 degree Celsius or even lower. Imagine a guy like me who had lived all my early life in a tropical country, suddenly thrust into a sub-zero temperature environment. *"Frozen Oliver"* would be the right description!

We were surprised to see a lot of Filipinos in Toronto. It was just like walking in our old neighborhood at times. We would hear casual Filipino, our national language, or even Ilonggo, the local dialect of the town that we came from. The influx of Filipino migrants was largely due to Canada's Caregiver Program that allowed caregivers to be a permanent resident after two years of working in the country. Caregivers endured real hardships though. Most were career professionals back home – some were teachers, accountants, engineers, etc. But they opted to take the Caregiver route, not only for themselves but for their families and especially their children. Other Filipino immigrants were nurses, IT specialists, dentists, doctors, and businessmen – all highly-skilled Filipino professionals.

New Spiritual Home

It was a new kind of experience for our family. Bea, who had just turned 12 at that time, adapted well to her school. She was not required to take English as a Second Language Class due to her proficiency. Watching cartoons when she was small and staying in the U.S. for eight months when she was five years old really helped her a lot. No wonder that in 2012 she got the School

Council Award for having the highest academic achievement in Language and Literature.

As for me, I was able to find a job after two weeks. I felt so blessed to at least have something to allow us to pay our rent, which was quite expensive, and to support our daily expenses. I could not be choosy about what kind of work I wanted. I just had to do what I needed to do to provide for my family.

But aside from the challenges of professional work, it was a smooth transition for us. Ena has an aunt and cousin who gave us a lot of support with everything. Auntie Judith and her husband Uncle Kim served as our second parents. They treated us as their own children. Renee Vic, Ena's cousin, and her husband Richard guided us through everything that immigrants needed to know about Toronto. God was so good to place people in our path and provide us with all the help we needed to survive.

We were also blessed to have Thornhill Baptist Church (TBC) as our spiritual home. They had a ministry that catered to the needs of Filipino caregivers and was later turned into a group that everyone could join. The same group provided us with support, bonding, and fellowship. TBC gifted us not only with a spiritual home but, through the kindness of its members, made our transition smooth and our stay a very meaningful one. We, as a family, assimilated to Canada's social dynamics pretty fast.

A Disheartening Welcome

In our third month in Toronto, however, robbers broke into our apartment. The culprits destroyed the door and mercilessly scattered our belongings all over the place while searching for valuables. All the things we considered valuable, which others might not see value in, were all taken away. I was just grateful that Ena was at school fetching Bea and I was at work. I could not, and don't want to, imagine what could have possibly happened if we had been there when the robbers broke into our abode.

My wife and daughter cried unabashedly when they arrived home. I had mixed emotions of fear, shock, and sadness. My heart was broken seeing my wife and daughter utterly dejected. I couldn't manage a word. We were helpless.

Although the robbery happened at about 3 P.M., the police didn't come until 4 A.M. the next day because it was not an emergency. With crushed hearts and a broken door, we gathered on the sofa and prayed. That was all we could do – and what God wanted us to do! It strengthened our faith. We hung on to His promises.

> "Be still before the LORD and wait patiently for Him; do not fret when men succeed in their evil ways, when they carry out their wicked schemes. Refrain from anger and turn from wrath; do not fret-it leads only to evil." *Psalm 37:7-8 (NIV)*

Two weeks after the robbery, I lost my job. Ena was only working for four hours a day, five days a week as a cleaner in a TV station. Life was really tough for us. We were struggling financially but I knew God was building us up spiritually. We continued to hang on to His promises.

> "But my God shall supply all your needs according to his riches in glory by Christ Jesus." *Philippians 4:19 (KJV)*

A lot of people back home assume that immigrating to Canada or other foreign countries automatically provides a better kind of life and a promised bounty. It's not so. Life in Canada was not easy. One needs perseverance, resiliency, forbearance, and Divine intervention to endure and survive. Many mistakenly get the impression when *balikbayans* go for vacation in the Philippines that they are very affluent. Maybe because some, in order to project an image of bounty, show off during their stay using their credit cards. They try to impress everyone, when in reality, they really do not have much.

Not everyone who lives and works in Canada or in another

country is wealthy. Many only earn enough for themselves and their families to sustain a decent life. While some might be financially well-off because of many years of hard work, a lot are struggling from pay check to pay check. However, in most developed foreign countries, hard workers can afford to have decent meals each day, buy their own houses, and send their kids to school. But for us who were new to the place, we were living one day at a time. We encountered a lot of challenges as we established our roots in Canada. God, however, never sleeps. He had His eyes and ears always open to anyone who seeks Him.

"The eyes of the LORD are toward the righteous and his ears toward their cry." *Psalm 34:15 (ESV)*

True enough, our good Lord did not forsake us during those troubled times.

New Connections

One of the Toronto Police officers who responded during the break in at our apartment was Officer Rene Mijares, a Philippine-born Canadian who hails from the province of Cebu. We had a chat and he explained why they had come so late. I fully understood and never really questioned how they did their job. I was once in the military service and most of the time we were swamped with tasks and could only do them one at a time. I have a soft spot in my heart for police officers, because I was in public service too. I never thought I would see Officer Mijares again.

A year after the incident, I received a phone call from him! He had my number because of our break in incident. He told me about a fellow officer of his who used to be with the Philippine Marines and knew somebody who graduated from the Philippine Military Academy. It was great news for me to have the new contact. I never expected to find like-minded people in Canada as I was too busy earning a decent living for my family.

Officer Mijares' call paved the way for me to connect with

the alumni of the Academy who had immigrated to Toronto. I was elated to talk to the guy Officer Mijares referred to me. Through him, I was introduced to Cav Jun Peñola, a member of PMA *"Maharlika"* Class of 1984 and who was the leader of the Philippine Marines group that regularly meets and has fellowships together on weekends. Through that connection, I was led to other groups of the Philippine Military Academy Alumni Association of Toronto (PMAAA-Toronto) under the leadership of Cav Clyde Claudio, a member of PMA *"Makabayan"* Class of 1975.

Living in Toronto had its own share of challenges. The cost of living is high and finding a good paying job was quite difficult. Canada, however, encourages the wealthiest around the world to immigrate by giving them business incentives, and the brightest by giving them opportunities to make it their home. The difficulty is that immigrants are required to have Canadian work-experience before they can work, and needed to attend Canadian schools to get their licenses in their respective careers. The challenge can be summed up in two practical questions, *"How can one have Canadian work experience when he has just arrived in the country?"* and *"How can one gain work experience when one is not allowed to work 'for lack of Canadian work history'?"*

Regardless, we applied and were allowed to immigrate to Canada because we were registered nurses. Although, we were not authorized to work as nurses or to practice our profession until we complete the assessment and registration process required by the College of Nurses of Ontario (CNO). We were not even allowed to take their licensure examination without first taking required subjects from Canadian nursing schools. Yes, surviving in our new found home was very challenging and we needed a lot of "strength" apart from our own.

New Mission

In 2012, I was given the opportunity to be a deacon at Thornhill Baptist Church (TBC). It was a humbling but spiritually rewarding experience since I had to deal with people from different cultures. The only common factor we had was Jesus Christ. I dealt with the routine things that surrounded the conduct of the church ministry. Ena continued to enjoy the blessing of being in the choir. Even still, we are so grateful to TBC for being our spiritual home for six fruitful years.

Then, in 2014, I was offered to make a presentation regarding Christianity and Ministry in the Philippines. During the presentation, a lot of folks were touched by my life's testimony and offered their partnership and participation. TBC donated $1,300 worth of Bibles for Highlight Fundamental Baptist Church (HFBC) in our hometown Alimodian, Iloilo, Philippines.

During our evangelical crusade in Iloilo in August 2014, several souls were brought to the feet of Jesus and countless were blessed and encouraged. I had the rare privilege of inviting former military colleagues to give their testimonies. They had found freedom in Jesus Christ in their respective struggles over the years. Among those who came to attend the event were: Ranger Geri Gambala, the valedictorian of our PMA Class '95 who is now an evangelist; Ranger Albert Baloloy, a trained U.S. Army Ranger who became a pastor; Ranger Boix Dingle, former commander of the 12th Scout Ranger (Always Ready) Company and who is heavily involved in church ministry; and Ranger Phil Fortuno, the former commander of 2nd Scout Ranger (Venceremos) Company who now spends most of his time in community development advocacy. It was an amazing moment to see those fearless warriors turned into faithful soldiers of the Lord Jesus Christ.

The evangelical crusade was culminated with a basketball exhibition game between the Alimodian Selection and Highlight Team reinforced by Ronald Tubid at the town's basketball gym. Ronald is a good friend of mine and a professional basketball player playing for San Miguel Beer in the Philippine Basketball Association (PBA) at that time. He was gracious enough to join the game, to the cheers of the crowd.

At the game's halftime, we preached the Word of God and shared a brief reflection on life and faith. The presence of Ronald was a blessing as it helped draw people to participate in the event. It was a fun and refreshing moment for everyone.

Finally, in 2016, after more than seven years of waiting, our US permanent resident visa applications were approved. As I looked back on the period it took us to eventually be allowed to immigrate to the United States, I could not help but remember God's promise to Sarah in the book of *Genesis 18:14, "Is anything too hard for the Lord?"*

Indeed, nothing is hard for Him for He is God. Truly, all things come about in His time – the perfect time.

•••••

Welcome to Canada. Arrival at Toronto Pearson International Airport (November 2010)

TBC Choir. Ena (second from right) with the Thornhill Baptist Church Music Ministry

Our Philippine Military Academy Alumni Association – Toronto (PMAAA – Toronto) Family

My Toronto Family. (Standing L-R) Kim Oliver and Uncle Kim (Seated L-R) Richard, Bea, Renee Vic, Rose, Aunte Judith, Ena and myself.

Soldiers for Christ. (Top row L-R) Ptr. Rehum Baldimor, myself, and Ranger Albert Baloloy. (Bottom row L-R) Ranger Boix Dingle, Ranger Geri Gambala, and Ranger Phil Fortuno.

Praying Before The Game. Ronald Tubid (#71), a member of San Miguel Team of the Philippine Basketball Association, joined us in a friendly game during the Evangelical Crusade. (August 2014)

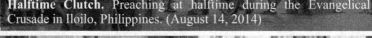

Halftime Clutch. Preaching at halftime during the Evangelical Crusade in Iloilo, Philippines. (August 14, 2014)

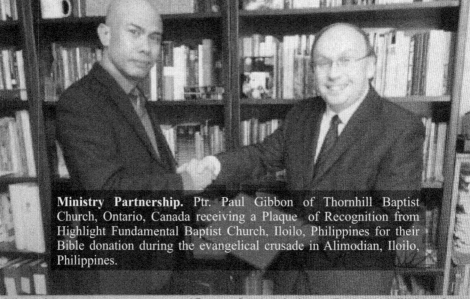

Ministry Partnership. Ptr. Paul Gibbon of Thornhill Baptist Church, Ontario, Canada receiving a Plaque of Recognition from Highlight Fundamental Baptist Church, Iloilo, Philippines for their Bible donation during the evangelical crusade in Alimodian, Iloilo, Philippines.

Oliver Almonares presents a certificate of appreciation to Rev. Paul Gibbon from

Church Camp. Fellowship with Community for Christ's Disciples led by Ptr Johnny Dalisay. (September 2016)

Friends in Christ. (Standing L-R) Yolly Korten,Ena, Beverly Bacomo, Claire Ramirez, myself, Bea, and Yamie Pacificar. (Seated L-R) Marshall Homecgoy, Jezebel Homecgoy, and Divina Ramos. (Canada Day – July 1, 2012)

Our TBC Family

CHAPTER **10**

CLUTCH TIME

"I am the vine, you are the branches;
he who abides in Me and I in Him, he bears much fruit,
for apart from Me you can do nothing."

— *Joshua 15:5 (NASB)*

A "clutch performance" in sports is a phenomenon that occurs to athletes under pressure in the crucial moments of a game. Usually, those are last minutes of a game when athletes manage to rise to the occasion, and summon the strength and focus necessary to succeed.

Being a "clutch player" is not an instant thing. It is a result of long and hard training, repetitive practices of possible scenarios, and resiliency in enduring the challenging process of preparation. The epitome of "Mr. Clutch" for me is Michael Jordan. My call sign when I was a company commander was "Jordan Six". I chose that for obvious reasons. Later on, Jordan was followed by another clutch player, Kobe Bryant.

I don't know much about other sports so I tend to take my examples from the game of basketball. Both athletes mentioned claimed that they practiced long and hard in order to reach the point where they could perform in clutch situations when the need arose. They have a passion that many other players do not have. They practice more than the others. They value winning more than the rest.

The Scout Rangers feel the same. They train harder than the ordinary soldier. They are motivated more than others. They have that passion for service more than the rest. I may be wrong about this, but somehow that's the Scout Ranger mindset, and it is necessary in order to do things that others do not want or are scared to do, or to go places where others have failed to go. That's the mindset that catapulted some of my fellow Scout Rangers to be awarded the highest combat medal, The Medal of Valor, for conspicuous acts of valor above and beyond the call of duty. In fact, the FSRR – as a unit – has the most number of Medal of Valor winners to this day.

I have made a few "clutch" baskets while playing competitive basketball. I sank some of them, but missed a lot as well. Shooting baskets in a tense situation requires a lot of skill and composure. As a Scout Ranger, I was just a mediocre officer in comparison to those who went ahead of us and those who followed behind. On top of my list of clutch performers is of course the most popular Scout Ranger, my former Regiment Commander, Lieutenant General Julius Javier, a proud member of PMA "*Matatag*" Class of 1970. His daring exploits and unsurpassed combat accomplishments earned for him the monicker "Living Legend."

The legends of the Scout Rangers continue. Here are the Scout Rangers who were awarded the Philippine highest combat award, the Medal of Valor:

In 1955, **Master Sergeant Francisco Camacho Jr.** was handpicked by his unit commander Colonel Ernesto Mata, who later become the AFP Chief of Staff and Secretary of Defense, to execute "Operation Secret." It was an intelligence mission that aimed to neutralize *Hukbong Laban sa Hapon (Hukbalahap)* leader Eddie Villapando. Upon the defeat of the Japanese, the Huk members remained insurgents and fought government forces. Villapando's group was sowing terror in Cavite, Laguna, and Batangas.

According to a *Catanduanes Tribune* article, Camacho and Corporal Weene Martillana had posed as civilians and managed to befriend Villapando and his bodyguards. Then, on December 20, 1955, Rangers Camacho and Martillana neutralized Villapando and his bodyguards. Unfortunately, Ranger Camacho died from a gunshot wound that he sustained during the encounter that happened along the highway between San Pablo City and Calauan town in Laguna. Camp Francisco Camacho in Virac, Catanduanes is named after him.

Corporal Wenee Martillana, was the audacious Ranger-buddy of Msg Camacho when they executed "Operation Secret". Ranger Martillana survived the December 20, 1955 encounter against the Hukbalahap leader Eddie Villapando. He went on to have a distinguished career in the military. A Bicolano like Msg Camacho, Ranger Martillana was highly honored by the AFP after naming a camp – Camp Weenee Martillana in Pili, Camarines Sur – after him.

Corporal Romualdo Rubi is a member of SR Class 63-84. A feature on the AFP website recalls that Rubi managed to fight off at least 100 heavily armed communist rebels who attacked a military detachment in Claver, Surigao del Norte on March 18, 1991. The write-up noted: "Succeeding investigations revealed that Rubi neutralized 26 of the rebels. The rest scuttled away after realizing that they could not take down the lone Ranger at the port despite their numerical advantage." Ranger Rubi would later on be commissioned as an Army officer and would eventually retire with the rank of Major.

On January 13, 1995, **Captain Cirilito Sobejana**, a member of PMA "*Hinirang*" Class 1987 and SR Class 109-92, and his men were fighting the Abu Sayyaf in Basilan. A Rappler feature by Carmela Fonbuena recalled: "The firefight apparently alerted other Abu

Sayyaf fighters until the enemies had swelled to 150." Despite being wounded, Sobejana carried on. He sustained a total of five gunshot wounds, one of which shattered his right forearm. His men attested that he maneuvered around and exposed himself to enemy fire in order to to direct the battle and operate the radio. They were able to hold off the enemy – killing 30 – for four hours until reinforcements arrived. Captain Sobejana is now a Major General and commands the Philippine Army's 6th Infantry (Kampilan) Division in Central Mindanao

Captain Edward *"Bakal"* Lucero, PMA *"Hinirang"* Class of 1987 and SR Class 92-88 was killed in action while serving as the commander of the 6th Scout Ranger (Cutting Edge) Company in 2000. He fought MILF rebels in Carmen town in Cotabato. "While defending the government's infrastructure project in the area, Lucero paid the ultimate sacrifice but showed the finest traditions of Filipino soldiery," wrote Harold Cabunoc in his article for *The Philippine Star*. Captain Lucero earned the nickname *"Bakal,"* which means "Steel," from his troops out of respect for his audacity in combat and for his frontline leadership.

Sergeant Claudio Forrosuelo was a member of the 8th Scout Ranger (*Destruere Hostis Deus*) Company, 2nd Scout Ranger Battalion who was KIA in Matanog, Maguindanao on May 3, 2000. A Rappler report by Mick Basa recalled: "Forrosuelo was deployed in Matanog, Maguindanao during the height of hostilities in the area. He was killed in a tactical assault against some 500 MILF rebels." Ranger Forrosuelo led a tactical assault on the enemy so that wounded soldiers could be evacuated. To make sure that his fellow soldiers could get out of the area, he, along with five others, chose to stay behind to keep fighting against a numerically-superior enemy. Ranger *"Porog'* – as he was fondly called by his peers and colleagues in the FSRR – is a proud member of SR Class 83-86.

2ⁿᵈ Lieutenant Herbert Dilag, PMA *"Masinag"* Class of 1998 and SR Class 135-99, led a "suicide squad" in Basilan in 2000. He was part of Oplan Final Option as a platoon leader of the 11ᵗʰ Scout Ranger (*Pericoloso*) Company. In late April 2000, they were tasked to clear four clusters of the Abu Sayyaf territory in Basilan. A Rappler feature written by Fonbuena explained: "They were to attack the notorious Hill 898 inside Camp Abdurajak – the slopes defended by the men of second-generation leader Khadaffy Janjalani. They were holding 28 civilian hostages. Dilag and his men were able to secure the northeast tip of Hill 898, the first of four clusters the entire team went there to take."

Sergeant Lucio Curig, a member of SR Class 51-83, was one of the 14 Rangers who volunteered for the "suicide squad" organized by 2Lt Herbert Dilag. They fought in an intense bunker-to-bunker, close quarter battle for four hours until they drove out the enemy. In that brutal battle, Ranger Curig highly exemplified the resolve of a Scout Ranger to fulfill his mission and sworn duty.

Lieutenant Colonel Noel Buan, PMA *"Maharlika"* Class of 1984 and SR Class 64-84, is from 1SRB. In an article published by in the *Visayas Daily Star*, Gilbert Bayoran wrote: "Buan was conferred the MOV for acts of conspicuous courage, gallantry, and intrepidity at the risk of life, above and beyond the call of duty during the almost two hours of encounter against Abu Sayyaf bandits in Lantawan, Basilan, on April 8, 2004." He added: "Despite his right hand being injured, Buan rallied his men to sustain the fight, to the extent of engaging the bandit group, headed by Hamsiraji Sali and his brother, Sahir, in hand-to-hand combat. Before the gun battle, Buan risked his life and posed as bait so that bandits will engage them in a firefight." Lt Col Buan would later retire as a Brigadier General in the AFP.

Private First Class Ian Pacquit, a member of of the 3rd Scout Ranger (Terminator) Company was KIA during the Zamboanga City Siege in 2013. Jorge Cariño of *ABS-CBN News* wrote: "Paquit first sustained an injury during a gun battle between government forces and MNLF rebels in Zamboanga City on September 13, 2013. Despite the injury, Ranger Paquit still went back to the frontline in Barangay Santa Barbara. Then, on September 24, four days before the siege ended, heavy exchange of fire trapped soldiers of the 3SRC in their position. Paquit decided to adjust his position to provide cover fire for the repositioning troops whose cover was deteriorating because of heavy enemy fire from an estimated 100 MNLF fighters." The troops were able to reposition at a point where there was minimal enemy resistance. Sadly, Ranger Paquit was shot in the neck and died.

Captain Rommel "Daredevil" Sandoval, a member of PMA *"Sanlingan"* Class of 2005 and SR Class 165-07, was KIA in the Battle of Marawi while serving as the commander of the 11th Scout Ranger (*Pericoloso*) Company. On September 10, 2017, he was killed while trying to save Corporal Jayson Mante. When Cpt Sandoval saw that the latter was hit, he ordered his men to provide cover fire as he ran to Mante. In her Rappler report, Natashya Gutierrez cited the accounts of Sandoval's men. She wrote: "As the bullets came flying in, Sandoval, in his last moments, was still thinking of his men. He crawled on top of Mante to shield him from getting hit further. When they recovered Sandoval's body, bullets were lodged in his chest. His body had blocked bullets from going through and hitting Mante."

These are the only ones I will mention. There is a long list of notable Scout Rangers who served and continue to serve our beloved country. The truth is, we are all trained to perform well in "clutch" situations, and by the grace of God, we accomplish the task when the situation calls for it.

I'm just grateful and blessed to be associated with this rare breed of men. I used to think that I was like them, courageous under fire, composed in the heat of the battle. But I was not, to be honest.

For many years, I thought I was responsible for my clutch performance but it has become obvious that I was not. The only reason I was able to survive those battles was because of God's overwhelming grace. The real "Clutch player" in my life is Jesus Christ; I just didn't see it before. Many people claim too much credit for themselves. But even the righteousness we claim is "filthy rags" in His sight *(Isaiah 64:6)*. An old hymn written by Edward Mote, a pastor at Rehoboth Baptist Church in Horsham, West Sussex in 1834 says it well:

> "My hope is built on nothing less
> Than Jesus' blood and righteousness
> I dare not trust the sweetest frame
> But wholly lean on Jesus' name
> On Christ the solid Rock I stand,
> All other ground is sinking sand."

Indeed, ALL other ground is sinking sand.

Unravelling

The Burnham Rescue might have been accomplished by human hands but it was really part of God's plan to reveal Himself. Foremost, despite it being a tragedy from the world's perspective, God used it to accomplish His purposes.

Through Gracia's story, a lot of people have been encouraged in their faith. No amount of human strength could overcome such a magnitude of hardships and challenges. She became an internationally sought after speaker and best-selling author.

Gracia's story of unimaginable forgiveness towards her captors is beyond human understanding. Her unconditional support to the children of her captors is unbelievable. Her passion to reach out to the Moro people is heart-warming. With an imperfect human heart, these things are impossible. "With man this is impossible, but with God all things are possible." *Matthew 19:26 (NIV)*. Truly, God achieved His purposes through her life.

After the rescue, God continued to mold me piece by piece into the person He wanted me to be. The Apostle Paul said it well when he encouraged the believers at Philippi saying,

> "Being confident of this very thing, that He who has begun a good work in you will complete it until the day of Jesus Christ." *Philippians 1:6 (NKJV)*

Indeed, God will continue to work on me until He achieves what He wants in my life. What came next in my life made the main purpose of my existence clear to me.

Reason for Being

"Why am I Here?" is a question we often ask from time to time. We wonder if there is something beyond what we see and feel. It evokes a lot of other questions and answers alike.

Dr. Rick Warren in his best-selling book, The Purpose Driven Life, puts it this way:

> Why on earth am I here?

> **Worship** – We were planned for God's pleasure. "You are worthy, our Lord and God, to receive glory and honor and power, for you created all things, and by your will they were created and have their being." *Revelation 4:11 (NIV);*

Fellowship – We were formed for God's family. "So in Christ Jesus you are all children of God through faith, for all of you who were baptized into Christ have clothed yourselves with Christ." *Galatians 3:26-27 (NIV);*

Discipleship – We were created to become like Christ. "Therefore, be imitators of God, as beloved children. And walk in love, as Christ loved us and gave himself up for us, a fragrant offering and sacrifice to God." *Galatians 5:1 (ESV);*

Ministry – We were shaped for serving God. "For we are God's handiwork, created in Christ Jesus to do good works, which God prepared in advance for us to do." *Ephesians 2:10 (NIV);* and,

Evangelism – We were made for God's mission. "Go therefore and make disciples of all nations, baptizing them in the name of the Father and of the Son and of the Holy Spirit, teaching them to observe all that I have commanded you. And behold, I am with you always, to the end of the age." *Matthew 28:19-20 (ESV).*

The big idea is Jesus Christ commissioned us.

A commission is an instruction or command. When I graduated from PMA in 1995, I was commissioned as a Second Lieutenant of the Armed Forces of the Philippines. As an officer, I was commanded to accomplish the mission of defending the freedom of my country to the best of my ability at any point in time. In so doing, I might have to make the ultimate sacrifice – to die, if need be – in fulfilling my commission. I did that for eight years with the Scout Rangers, a well-trained unit composed of "clutch players."

As I have grown in my faith and become closer to Jesus Christ, I realized that if I am willing to serve and even die for my country, what prevents me from doing the same for the Creator of this universe?

"In the beginning God created the heavens and the earth."
Genesis 1:1 (NIV)

And because He is the creator, He owns everything, and He makes the rules.

We have to know who God is and why He sent His Son Jesus. God is perfect. But we are not. "All have sinned and fall short of the glory of God" *Romans 3:23*. Sin separated us from God. We needed reconciliation, so He sent His Son Jesus to redeem us,

"For God so loved the world that He gave His only Son, that whoever believes in him should not perish but have eternal life." *John 3:16 (ESV)*.

People seem to be very uncomfortable when we talk about hell. The truth is, God loves us so much that He gave us the choice to believe. Otherwise we would perish. People lean so much on God's unconditional love, but often neglect the fact that God is also just. Justice must be served. Jesus made the perfect sacrifice. We just have to accept God's offer of forgiveness. By the way, this is not my concept. It is God's word.

When you know who God is and why you were created, then you start to live a life that is not dependent on yourself. You do not rely on your human abilities anymore but you cling to Him.

Like in sports and special military operations, to be ready to perform well in a spiritual clutch, you need a lot of repetitive study of His Word. So that when the clutch time comes, you will respond in the right way with the guidance of the Holy Spirit.

Going Stateside

I immigrated to the United States from Canada in October 2016.

My wife and daughter moved a month before. I made sure that she settled first before I resigned from my job at Toronto Western Hospital.

On the day of their flight, they expected the Canada immigration officer to check their sealed immigration papers, but he did not. So my wife thought maybe their papers would be inspected once they arrived in Chicago. When they arrived there, they went directly to claim their baggage. She wondered who would check their immigration papers. In good faith, she tried to look for an immigration officer to present her case. The officer told them they should have been submitted to the U.S immigration officer in Toronto, Canada. Since they are already in Chicago, the officer said he would take care of the paperwork and update their system.

When it was my time to fly a month later, my wife told me to make sure that I give my papers to the immigration officer in Toronto. And so I did. As soon as the officer opened my sealed envelope and looked up our case on his computer he asked me.

"Where are your wife and daughter?" He seemed concerned.

I said, *"In Chicago."*

"How did they get there?"

"By plane."

"What's their point of entry?"

"Chicago."

He picked up the phone and after the call he instructed me.

"Take your seat there and wait."

I waited patiently for about an hour. I saw him going back and forth in the office. He was talking with another guy who seemed to be his supervisor. They were looking at me as I was using my phone to coordinate with my brother who would be picking me up at O'Hare Airport in Chicago. The supervisor yelled at me, *"Don't use your phone!"*

I really didn't know what was happening. Then the officer who was checking my papers called me.

"I'm going to re-seal your papers. If you want to enter the United States, you have to call your wife to fetch you here."

You see, my wife was the main applicant and I was her dependent. He explained that my wife should have submitted the papers to them. I explained that she wanted to, but no one asked for it. They entered the United States using their Canadian Permanent Resident cards. He insisted that there was no other way. I countered that maybe I could enter the U.S. as a Canadian citizen but he said, *"No, because I already know that you are entering as a U.S immigrant."* He was so firm that I could not enter the U.S in the present situation.

I excused myself to go to the washroom. I had to borrow the key because it was locked. I went to the washroom to send text messages to my brother about my situation so that they wouldn't be waiting for me at Chicago airport. Then I prayed, *"Lord, you brought me this far in my life. You could have taken my life many times but you chose to spare me and work things out in my life. I believe you have a plan for me. That's why you continue to extend your grace and mercy. I really don't believe you're going to drop me at this time. You are in control."* And I recited a very powerful Scripture verse that says,

> "Be still and know that I am God. I will be exalted among the nations. I will be exalted in the earth." *Psalm 46:10 (NIV)*

"Lord, whatever you want, let it be. I'll follow you," I surrendered my U.S. dream right at that point. He knew what was best for me and for my family. I just had to trust His plan and obey His will – nothing more, nothing less.

When I got back from the washroom, the immigration officer handed me my papers. I was thinking about the things we had planned upon my arrival to the United States – the scheduled vacation I had planned, and a lot of other things which now had become almost impossible.

The Immigration officer firmly told me, *"The only way for you to enter the U.S. is for your wife to come back to Canada and take you back with her. No other way. Any questions?"*

I sheepishly answered, *"None, sir"*. Then I picked up my papers.

As I was about to turn my back he asked me again, *"Did your wife and daughter get their Permanent Resident Cards?"*.

I said, *"Yes"*.

"Can you tell your wife to send pictures of their PR (Permanent Residency) *cards to my e-mail?"* Then he wrote his e-mail on a sticky note paper.

I was tempted to smile but I maintained my composure. I thought, *"Test of faith. You are a great God."*

I asked the Immigration officer, *"Can I call her instead?"*

"Yes, you can use your phone now", he instructed.

In a few minutes, he had what he wanted. He took my immigration papers and politely told me, *"You may go. Sorry for the inconvenience."*

"Thank you, sir!", I responded with a smile. I almost saluted and hugged him in sincere gratitude!

I only had 15 minutes to catch up with my scheduled flight. I ran as fast as I could. I was the last one to board the plane. Just in time.

Whew!

While sitting on the plane, I thought about what had just transpired. The Immigration officer was just doing his job. It may be that the immigration officers on duty at the time of my wife's and daughter's entry to the U.S. had forgotten to take care of their paperwork. As for me, I opted not to say much and allowed God's sovereignty to take over. Obviously, the officer's heart had softened and he eventually became reasonable, and compassionate. I certainly couldn't claim any credit for that because I never even tried to talk things out with him.

What I experienced with the Immigration officer was no doubt God's intervention. He was telling me to cherish the opportunities I may have henceforth. That was a great example of God's coming through in a "clutch moment" where we needed Him most. I was overwhelmed with gratitude.

Truly, a sovereign God – He is the ultimate "clutch player"!

•••••

Grateful. Arrived at Chicago O'Hare International Airport after being procedurally held by an Immigration Officer in Toronto for almost three hours. (October 16, 2016)

Control and Composure. Controlling the game during the Jurado Cup 2015 in Waukegan, Illinois. (September 2015)

Most Valuable Player. Receiving the MVP award for Basketball during the Jurado Cup 2015 closing ceremony. (L-R) Cavalier Rory Hormillosa, PMAAA Midwest President (Class '78), myself, and Cavalier Murdie Olan (Class '79)

Clutch Free Throw. Making the crucial shot that sealed the win during the Jurado Cup 2017 in Virginia, USA. (September 2017)

(L-R) Cav. Murdie Olan ('79), Cav. Sam Sy ('82), myself, Cav. Riego de Dios ('81), Cav. Herold Ochoco ('81)

Team Chicago. Philippine Athletic Sports Association (PASA) Tournament held in Queens, New York participated by various teams from other states in the US. I was wearing jersey #2. (July 2017)

Men of God at the VOM Conference. (L-R). Pastor Hector Palacios from Indiana, a missionary with a ministry in Zamboanga City, and Prof. Arnold Quitevis, my PMA upperclassman ('83), a retired US serviceman and also a pastor. (October 2017)

The Nightingale. With Helen Berhane, gospel singer, speaker and author who was imprisoned in a container van for almost two years in her native Eritrea in Africa because of her Christian faith. Her story is told in her book, "Song of the Nightingale". (VOM, October 2017)

Labor Camp Survivor. With Sarah Liu, speaker and author of the book, "Sarah's Journey of Faith". She was imprisoned in a labor camp in China for almost six years because of her Christian faith. (VOM, October 2017)

VOM Conference at Morton, Illinois. (L-R) Ptr. Bob Garcia, Gracia Burnham, and myself. (June 2018)

Champion Life Centre Visit. Attended the Champion Life Centre in Scarborough, Ontario, Canada. (L-R) Leo Fabila, Amy Fabila, Bick Mendoza-Miller, Ena Almonares, myself, and Rev. Jerry Berenguer. (June 2016)

My Upperclassman. My PMA upperclassman, Rev. Jerry Berenguer (Class '81), Senior Pastor, Champion Life Centre Canada. (June 2016)

Clutch for Christ. Giving my testimony during the Filipino Community Baptist Church anniversary in Woodridge, Illinois. (November 2018)

CHAPTER 11

ALL THINGS WORK TOGETHER FOR GOOD

"And we know that God causes all things to work together for good to those who love God, to those who are called according to His purpose."

— *Roman 8:28 (NASB)*

I really like the story of Joseph in the Bible (Genesis Chapters 37-50). I always use it as an example every time I share about God's sovereignty. It is a classic illustration of how God works things out to achieve His purposes amidst the many complexities of human life.

One has to read the whole story to have a full understanding of what I'm talking about. For those who are not so familiar with the story, here's the summary.

Joseph was the 11th son of Jacob, who had twelve sons (the twelve tribes of Israel came from these men). Joseph was sold by his brothers out of jealousy and he ended up as a slave in Egypt. His brothers then told their father that Joseph was devoured by a ferocious animal. They showed their father Joseph's coat of many colors soaked in blood as evidence. The blood, however, was not Joseph's but that of an animal. His life was hard in Egypt but by Divine Providence, he became a trusted leader of the Pharaoh.

After some years, there was a famine in the land of Canaan, where Jacob and his sons lived. They came to Egypt to buy grain, as it was the only place where there was an abundance of food during that time. They did not know that Joseph was now a trusted leader under Pharaoh. Joseph tested his brothers but eventually he revealed himself. This is what he said to them.

"You intended to harm me, but God intended it all for good. He brought me to this position so I could save the lives of many people" *Genesis 50:20 (NLT)*

Consequently, Joseph brought his family to his house in Egypt to be with him. There were 70 of them when they came to Egypt. They multiplied and were later known as the Israelites, from the word Israel (another name for Jacob).

I am so overwhelmed to think of how God continually works things out in the lives of billions of people in this world in addition to sustaining the intelligent design of the universe. If God can do all of these complicated processes beyond our limited human understanding, then surely He is in total control of ALL things despite how it appears from our human perspective. The more we appreciate God's overwhelming sovereignty, the more we see ourselves as desperately needing it. It's a very humbling realization. God asked Job a very sobering question,

"Where were you when I laid the foundation of the earth? Tell me, if you have understanding." *Job 38:4 (ESV)*

Rebound

After the Oakwood Incident in July 27, 2003, I decided to leave the military service with a heavy heart. I was doing fairly well but I made poor choices and was suffering the consequences of that. A lot of people thought I could have done more had I remained in the military service. Looking back now, I don't have negative emotions but rather, my heart is full of gratitude. God allowed me and my family to experience the "rock bottom" in our lives so we would be closer to Him. It was a humbling experience for me to start again from nothing and be void of the influence and power that I used to have. I learned to know who GOD really is and fully understood that Jesus Christ is not only my Savior, but He is most of all my Lord. God taught me what it means "to serve". Military service was just a preparation for me to serve the Commander-in-Chief of this universe.

"Just as the Son of Man did not come to be served but to serve, and to give his life as a ransom for many."
Matthew 20:28 (NKJV)

My wife and I decided to volunteer our services to the church ministry without hope of financial gain, or recognition. Together, we soldiered on knowing everything was preparation for future battles that would await us in life.

Submit and Follow

On July 9, 2016, I had the privilege of being invited to speak with Gracia Burnham in Toronto hosted by The New Tribes Mission, now known as Ethnos Canada and Ontario Filipino Ministerial Fellowship (OFMF). *Ethnos* means ethnicities in Greek. OFMF is a fellowship of Filipino churches in the province of Ontario, Canada.

I was so blessed to see her again after 13 years. When I was introduced by Gracia, the audience was in awe and disbelief. How in the world was it possible for a person involved in her rescue to be with her in Toronto? It was like another piece of the puzzle of her story (and mine as well) was put into place. It was also a memorable experience for my family to meet her for the first time.

Also gracing the occasion was Gracia's friend, Bick Mendoza Miller, who had made a trip to the Philippines in order to relay Gracia's message of forgiveness to the imprisoned terrorists in the maximum security prison in Muntinlupa, Philippines.

She narrated the events of her visit to meet with the terrorist kidnappers who are incarcerated. According to her, four of those convicted terrorists are now believers in Jesus Christ attending Bible studies inside the prison. From the human perspective, it is impossible, "*but with God all things are possible*." Our reunion manifested God's overwhelming sovereignty.

•••

Transitioning to a life in the United States of America is indeed challenging. But with the support of my family in Illinois, I experienced God's indescribable grace and mercy. Through the help of some friends with their recommendations, my wife and I were able to have full time jobs as Registered Nurses (RN) despite our lack of U.S. work experience. Indeed, He touched people's hearts to make things happen for our good and His glory.

To survive and live well in a foreign land entails determination, perseverance, humility and a doable plan of action – aside from constantly seeking guidance from the Lord Almighty. One must reasonably accept the fact that moving to a new place means a limited, if not inexistent, support system. Hence, ingenuity and steadfastness come in handy.

My military training and experience, particularly being a Scout Ranger, was a huge help to us. I, being the head of the family, needed to stay the course and keep faith that - with His blessing - we will overcome, though not immediately but definitely, all the challenges in the long run. As a Scout Ranger, I learned to survive alone and to survive anything thrown at me. I knew that everything was temporary, even hardships. The only thing that is constant is *change*, and Him.

Also, my training in the PMA became a solid anchor amid the many trials I encountered during and after my years in the military service, particularly after we immigrated to foreign lands. My journey into the military life started when I entered the PMA as a young cadet – a fourthclassman or a plebe. During my 1st year in the Academy, we plebes were taught so many "knowledges" that most young men would have a hard time digesting in their minds. But one among the many "knowledges" that struck me and stayed in my mind was a prayer that became a solid anchor to me over the years, especially in my times of doubt and adversity. It was the Cadet's Prayer, and I quote:

"Grant us, Oh God, that we may worship Thee to the utmost of faith and the limits of truth and suffer us not to fail to see the light of our true religion. Guide us that we may live this life to the fullest in devotion to Thee, in service to humanity and country and in the realization of our true self. Let the light of Thy divine wisdom direct us to a firm resolve to live up at all times to the creeds of our institution and teach us never to fail to measure up to the ideals of the profession we have chosen through life to follow. Make us do or think or say of others that which we want done, or thought, or said of us. Help us to live each day in the passing years in useful efforts that our lives may be spent in accord with the pattern of our creeds -the true, the noble, and the high. Give us that honest purpose in life which seeks fair deal with everyone and spurns all forms of hypocrisy that will enkindle our fighting faith, and smother all seeds of cowardice and fear in our hearts; the loyalty to our principles that places all issues above personal considerations, and shuns compromise with vice and injustice. Strengthen our hearts with fortitude that we may discipline our lives to trail the difficult paths rather than to stray on the easier ways. Teach us to aspire above the levels of common lives. Help us to see all things in their true light that we may guard against the frivolity in the sacred things of life even as we may enjoy in clear laughter its many delights. Teach us to make our play in every game, whether in mere sports or in life's mightier struggles, one where our desire to win is second only to our love of the game itself, where we triumph as considerate victors or lose with grace and a determined will to win. Endow our hearts with kindness that we may sympathize with those who sorrow and suffer; unite us in friendship, with all and help us share the merriment of those with cheerful countenance that we may partake of their joy. All of which we ask with faith to the everlastingness of Thine fount of grace to all men. Amen."

The Cadet's Prayer never failed to uplift my spirit whenever I recite it – a tremendous source of spiritual vigor to me.

And sometimes, I also took counsel, and got a good laugh, from the encompassing wisdom of one of our precious plebe knowledges "How is the Soldier?" – which I ask and funnily answer it myself too,

"Sir, from the weather – beaten terrains of Babuyan Islands to the streaming jungles of Tawi-tawi, the Filipino soldier stands as the proud guardian of his country and people.

He is the living prototype of all that is noble in the stealth and skill of a black panther stalking its prey, in the killer instinct and fighting heart of sea-borne warriors in the heat of battle, in the courage and determination of a professional prize fighter during a world championship bout and in the chivalry and compassion of a knight-in-shining armor to a fallen enemy.

He is awestruck and dumbfounded by the magnanimous duty that the people has bestowed upon him. The duty that binds the soldier to be the protector of the free, the duty that drives him to endure days without food, traverse all inhospitable terrain, through typhoons and searing rays of the sun, the duty that dislocates his normal life, separates him from his family, live with humble means and simple ways and be the epitome of the ideals of Courage, Integrity and Loyalty. Nonetheless, the iridescent rays from the Almighty Creator and the undying love of his people gives the soldier the strength of a thousand supernovas not to shirk that duty.

In short and simple language, the Filipino soldier will defend his country and people till his atoms are scattered to infinite void of the universe, Sir!"

Quitting in life? No...never. Thank you, PMA. Thank you, dear God!

Voice of the Martyrs

Then, fast forward to October 23, 2017. I had the privilege of attending the Voice of the Martyrs Conference in Chesterton, Indiana, USA which was just an hour drive from home. Selected speakers from all over the world gave their testimonies of God's goodness amidst persecution that almost cost them their lives. It was empowering to hear the life and death experiences of those who are spreading the love of God through Jesus Christ on the frontlines of spiritual warfare around the globe.

Gracia Burnham represented the Philippines as she told her horrifying experiences of being kidnapped by the Abu Sayyaf terrorists for more than a year, and how God miraculously worked things out for her to see her family again. I saw and felt that the audience were touched by her testimony. Everyone was all eyes and ears on Gracia. Suddenly, in the middle of her speech, she requested that I stand and be acknowledged. I was not prepared for that since I had just gone to listen and be inspired by the stories of some heroes of the faith. I felt awkward but Gracia encouraged me to embrace it, for it is God's will.

What happened after the event surprised me even more! People asked me to sign Gracia's books. The same thing had happened in Toronto. I hesitated because they were not my books. In my life, I never would have thought of doing something like that. But the people waiting in line would say, "We want you to sign as well", Gracia would just look at me with a smile and nod of approval. Some requested a video of me greeting their Filipino church congregation. Others asked me to pray for them right there! It was humbling to be used by God in many ways, despite my flaws and not being deserving.

As I remembered that moment on that desolate ridge of Culasian, Sirawai, Zamboanga del Norte while waiting for the rescue helicopters on June 7, 2002, I could not have had any idea as to what God was going to do with my life. Some events in life may be tragic from the human perspective but God is always able to "work things out for good" somehow.

> "And we know that all things work together for good to them that love God, to them who are the called according to His purpose." *Romans 8:28 (KJV)*

This is the New Testament version of *Genesis 50:20*, when Joseph revealed himself to his brothers.

•••

I have always liked the number 7. It is the number of God's completion. I was born on the 7th of July (7th month) 1970, 07/07/70. It was on the 7th of June that the rescue happened. It took us 7 years to immigrate to Canada after my military service. It was 7 long years before our US visa was approved. It took me 7 years to finally decide to write this book.

I'm actually a believer in Jesus Christ and I don't believe in numerology. I am just in awe when I realize God's grace and mercy through the many milestones of my life. It's incomprehensible for many of us to understand the will of God, but it is in the lowest and hardest points in our lives that we can see clearly and feel Him the most. I like how the New Living Translation of the Bible says it,

"My thoughts are nothing like your thoughts", says the LORD. "And my ways are far beyond anything you could imagine." *Isaiah 55:8 (NLT)*

With this, it brings us to another hard truth. God said to Moses,

"I will have mercy on whom I have mercy, and I will have compassion on whom I have compassion." *Romans 9:15 (NIV)*

When He forgives, it's beyond amazing.

"As far as the east is from the west. So far has He removed our transgressions from us." *Psalms 103:12 (NASB)*

How God works in our lives is beyond human comprehension, for He is God.

Seeking Spiritual Growth

The passion inside me to study more about the word of God has been so compelling. It's been lingering in my heart for a long time to pursue further studies. I fell in love with listening to sermons of great preachers and discussions in apologetics by the great theological minds. I prayed for many years wondering if further study was part of God's plan for my life.

So, in the fall of 2018, I finally enrolled at Moody Theological Seminary in Chicago and took up a Certificate in Biblical Studies. It is so humbling to be in the midst of Biblical scholars and be a part of this historical and evangelical institution. When I began, I felt like I knew nothing. Learning starts with a contrite heart, and by God's grace, through the power of the Holy Spirit, I have been able to be a good student. Having a full-time job, and doing school at the same time was very challenging and expensive, but it has been very fulfilling. Gracia generously helped me with my tuition as well. What a story!

I am just taking everything one day at a time. I've concluded that every decision within God's will is always the best decision. God brought me this far, and surely He will carry me through.

The way He works things out in our lives is like the bottom of the crochet. It appears messy and unattractive, but the other side – the finished product – is a thing of beauty.

> "But now, O LORD, you are our Father; we are the clay, and you are our potter; we are all the work of your hand."
> *Isaiah 64:8 (ESV)*

The Potter is sovereign and has the right to form or mold the clay in any way He wants. To give emphasis, I would like to share the mail-out letter from The Martin and Gracia Burnham Foundation:

Two Special People

I got a word several days ago that Musab was killed in a gun battle with the military (she was referring to the War in Marawi City in mid-2017 caused by the ISIS terrorists in the Philippines). Musab isn't his real name. It was his alias. His real name is Isnilon Hapilon. He was one of the "worst of the worst" and the final leader of those involved in our hostage situation to die (May 2001-June 2002), His day of grace is over. I feel so sad for him.

I happen to know Musab's future. Musab's knee will bow and Musab will confess that Jesus is Lord. (Revelation 20;11-15 and Philippians 2:9-11)

I've had lots of "closure-type" thoughts running thru my mind the last few days…so imagine my surprise when two of the men who did so much for Martin and me showed up at a Conference near Chicago. John Gray, the lead FBI investigator of our case, and Oliver Almonares, the commander of the Philippine Scout Rangers group that rescued us, had never met before. I couldn't believe that we were all there together. I couldn't have planned that if I tried!

As I prepared to speak, fiddling with my mic, etc., I glanced up and there was John and Oliver chatting away. So neat. I suddenly had a "vision" of one day, Martin, John, and Oliver in Heaven, talking, talking, talking about how our lives intersected, and what God did in the midst of that crazy, messy story!

God's ways are not our ways. He knows the end from the beginning. We only see the "now." And we can trust Him as He writes our stories.

Gracia Burnham

Truly amazing!

•••••

Our Second Reunion. All smiles in Toronto (July 2017)

Gracia introducing me as the Commanding Officer of the 15th Scout Ranger Company who was responsible for her rescue. The conference was organized by then New Tribes Mission Canada now known as Ethnos 360 in collaboration with the Ontario Filipino Ministerial Fellowship. (July 2017)

The Visit. Gracia visited our home on her way to speak for the Voice of the Martyrs Conference in Chesterton, Indiana, USA. (October 2017)

The Voice of the Martyrs Conference held in Chesterton, Indiana, USA. (L-R) myself, Gracia Burnham, and John Gray. (October 2017)

My CPU - DHS classmates in Illinois, USA. (L-R) Lorela, myself, Pressian, Jenie, Merliza, Leomarie, and Honey.

Celebrating Christmas with Matt Stott (leftmost) and his wife Angelica (3rd from left) – our family from Connecticut, USA.

Enjoying family bonding and fellowship. (Standing L-R) Jessie, Reyna, Sean, Linnea, Michelle, myself, and Ena. (Seated L-R) Asher, Macky, Virginia, Micah, and Jared.

Reunion in Illinois, USA. (Top row L-R) Jessie, Reyna, Sean, Helen, Virginia, Vinia, Michelle, Bev, Linnea. (Bottom row L-R) Ena, Jared, Micah, myself, Asher, Macky, and Rey.

CHAPTER 12

PRESS ON

"I press on toward the goal to win the prize for which
God has called me heavenward in Christ Jesus."

— Philippians 3:14 (NIV)

Nursing is defined as the protection, promotion, and optimization of health and abilities, prevention of illness and injury, facilitation of healing, alleviation of suffering through the diagnosis and treatment of human response, and advocacy in the care of individuals, families, groups, communities, and populations (American Nurses Association). The definition may sound fancy but in practice the Nursing profession does carry that huge responsibility.

"Special military operations" and "nursing" are no doubt two different things. Cleaning guns and "cleaning up" patients who can't fully take care of themselves have nothing in common. In the military, particularly in special operations, the objective is to neutralize the enemy by all means. Consequently, people get killed – soldiers and the enemies of the state alike – in the process. In nursing, the objective is to preserve the lives of patients and give them the optimum care necessary. These are two totally different fields.

•••

I never dreamed of becoming a nurse, but I became one anyway. I was influenced and led by the circumstances of life to be drawn into this profession through Divine Providence. At first, I thought it would be my means to achieve my goal to immigrate to the US. But as I was drawn into the Nursing profession, I realized that one couldn't remain in this field without genuine compassion. Nursing is a full commitment to compassion.

God uses people from all walks of life to reveal Himself. Nursing is very unique in that it provides an enormous platform to manifest personal care and have a healing ministry. People think that nursing in North America is good because of the pay. But one doesn't really realize how challenging it can be unless one wears those scrub suits. For example, my wife used to work in a rehabilitation center/nursing home providing care to a maximum of 34 elderly residents. Most of them were demented and some exhibited psychotic behavior. I can't imagine taking care of them. I would go nuts. But my wife, no doubt, is gifted in that area. She has tons of patience, compassion, and utmost commitment to the profession.

As for me, I once worked in a psychiatric unit handling ten patients. Most of them were schizophrenic, bipolar, depressed, suicidal, and homicidal for reasons that I don't know. Sadly, a lot of them abused street drugs and alcohol. Mental illness combined with street drugs and alcohol is very dangerous.

The challenges of nursing are not just dealing with the patients, but also with their families, and at times our own co-workers as well. A good nurse knows well how to balance stress, accomplish the tasks, and keep up good professional relationships in the workplace. One cannot function well without the other.

Dealing with patients' families is sometimes more challenging than the actual patients. Patient's families no doubt care for their loved ones and want the best for them. At times, nurses end up bearing the brunt of their frustrations and even their life issues. Nurses are commonly underrated or thought to be poor in terms of negotiation and crisis prevention skills. But actually, they are one of the best professionals.

Character-Defining Experience

I was blessed to have experienced both the military and nursing profession. Military life is regimented. There is a system. It requires discipline, and physical and mental toughness. Above all, it requires one to offer his life and to fully embrace the meaning of the word "sacrifice." The military for me is still the best organization to get things done efficiently in many ways.

On the other hand, nursing requires compassion and care. A nurse without these traits is miserable and will always be grumpy. Nursing doesn't normally require one to offer his or her life to accomplish the task.

For me, the challenge of nursing was very much different from that of the military. Patients demand and complain a lot. Co-workers complain as well. But despite these overwhelming challenges, I'm grateful because I became a better person through my nursing career. I've had this unique privilege to develop my character and be a channel of blessing not only to the patients but to those working with me.

Dr. David Jeremiah said in one of his sermons, "Reputation is what others know about us while character is what God knows about us". While it feels great to have a good reputation, I prefer to have a good character. In my work environment, it is hard to keep my composure while dealing with very difficult and irrational patients. But I praise and thank God for putting me in such a challenging situation to mold me into the person He wants me to be.

Lead Up Front

I work in a psychiatric ward. The patients are mentally sick. Five days a week, I deal with those challenges. Patients attack staff verbally and sometimes physically without provocation. A lot of them have their "own world", like in the movie "A Beautiful Mind" (2001). They are in the state of extreme depravity due to their delusions, hallucinations and many more of their psychotic tendencies. Such is their frame of mind and I understand them because they are controlled by their disease. Their rational thinking is affected.

The psychiatric ward is truly a different kind of battlefield, so to speak. Once, a co-worker of mine had a "black eye" after having been punched multiple times by a patient. Consequently, she was brought to the Emergency Room. She was not able to work for three months due to physical, psychological, and emotional trauma. She had to recover fully before going back to work. Cases like this have been reported and documented well, and they are part of the hazards of the nursing profession. Yes, a lot of our staff have been victims of unprovoked patient attack. I've had my own share of verbal and violent physical attacks, too.

Patients sometimes destroy hospital property when they act out. They would hurt themselves with anything in order to get attention. One of our patients slammed his head into the glass window of our medication room. Lots of stories. But one stands out.

One day, a patient asked one of our chaplains to pray with him. As the chaplain started the prayer with closed eyes, the patient lifted her with his bare hands and slammed her into the wall. Then he punched her multiple times. As he slammed her, the panic button was pressed and the alarm signal went off. All available staff rushed to the scene to help. I was in another section of the unit dealing with a patient who was also acting out. As I ran towards the area, I could hear loud voices shouting, *"Stop! Stop!"* When I arrived at the scene, I saw one of the male staff trying his very best to pull the patient away from the chaplain. The patient kept on stamping the chaplain's head on the floor with his size 13' right foot! The patient was a young, athletic 6-foot 4-inch tall guy; while the almost 60-year old lady chaplain was skinny and petite (just over five feet tall).

Instinctively, I forcibly grabbed the patient's other arm and helped the male staff member drag the patient out of the room in order to facilitate the escape of the chaplain. The delusional patient claimed that the chaplain was responsible for killing his whole family. The chaplain was taken to the Emergency Room, where thankfully the CT head scan result of her head was normal.

Can you imagine the physical mismatch when the patient attacked the lady chaplain? The incident could have ended tragically had the patient not been restrained in a timely way.

As I pondered on that incident, I realized I was put in that unit for a reason. I felt a sense of purpose. Looking back, I got that job just two weeks after I arrived in the U.S. when a military colleague who became a nurse as well, graciously guided me in getting the job. I knew I was there for a good reason.

Onward Always

When I started to work in that hospital, I was struggling with almost everything. It was a very humbling situation. In those moments I had to depend on God for wisdom, strength, and sustenance. Nursing is a different 'battlefield' from what I was used to, and the enemy is myself. No one literally dies but the circumstances are still very challenging.

Sometimes in my moments of silence, I couldn't help but hum – in my head – the timeless and ever-meaningful hymn of PMA. The lyrics of "PMA, Oh Hail To Thee" captivated my heart from the day I learned of it, and it had become one of my steady source of inspiration over the years. How could I not be motivated by its powerful words?

> Oh, Proud and bold you stand
> Bright beacon of the land
> Let loyal sons proclaim
> Thy glorious name
> Wherever we may be

O'er land or deep blue sea
We'll raise a song for thee,
Academy oh hail to thee
At every end of day
We hope and fervent pray
The honor you instill
Doth guide our will
May thy sons ever be
Men of Integrity,
Courage and Loyalty
PMA oh hail to thee

When bells for us are rung
And our last taps is sung
Let generations see
Our country free
Oh lead to righteous way
Those solid ranks of gray
Thy virtues to display
Academy oh hail to thee

The composers - Cavaliers Quirico P. Evangelista and Reynaldo A. Mendoza, both proud members of PMA Class 1940 - had truly created a masterpiece that inspires everyone, particularly alumni of PMA, to excel in everything. Movingly, as the hymn goes, "...At every end of day, we hope and fervent pray, the honor you instill doth guide our will...May thy sons ever be men of Integrity, Courage and Loyalty..." so is my resolve, and by God's empowerment, be a channel of His blessing.

Patience and Compassion

Prior to my job in Chicago, I worked as a Patient Care Assistant (PCA) in Toronto, Canada for almost five years. I had the privilege of taking care of people from all walks of life while working at the Internal Medicine Unit and Emergency Departments. PCAs don't do much computer stuff or the complex procedures that nurses do. They work more with bedside care. What I liked about working as a PCA was that I got to interact more with the patients as I helped them with basic hygiene that they couldn't do because of their sickness. They would begin to trust you – and in the process, they open up their lives and worldviews.

In the politically correct society of North America, it is very challenging to share your faith. For me, sharing is a conversation. I always pray that God will give me an opportunity to share. Through my sincere acts of compassion and genuine care, patients usually take notice and start to ask questions. They wonder what motivates someone to do those things that they can't imagine themselves doing for others. Genuine compassion is always a good platform to open a deep conversation. I always start by explaining that nursing is not for everyone. As conversations get more and more interesting, we reach a time when we can talk about the serious and important things in this earthly life, and even eternal life. *1 Peter 3:15 (ESV)* says,

> "but in your hearts honor Christ the Lord as holy, always being prepared to make a defense to anyone who asks you for a reason for the hope that is in you: yet do it with gentleness and respect."

•••

In Mark Cahill's book "One Thing You Can't Do in Heaven," he explained why believers of Jesus Christ always win when we share our faith. There are three possibilities when we share our faith. First, the person can accept Jesus Christ; second, the person can reject Jesus Christ; and third, we can plant the seed. When we are instruments for a person to surrender his/her life to Jesus, that's definitely a win. When a person contemplates on what we have shared, we are planting a seed and that's a win. If we ever get rejected in the name of Jesus, we will be blessed and the glory of God will rest upon us. That's no doubt a win. 1 *Peter 4:14 (NIV) says,*

"If you are insulted because of the name of Christ, you are blessed, for the Spirit of glory and of God rests on you."

This win-win perspective greatly inspires me to share whenever opportunity arises.

When I was in Toronto, I took care of a patient who was bed-ridden. He was "skin and bones" as a result of a complicated disease. I always cleaned him up as he could hardly move. On the third day, he engaged me in a meaningful conversation. We talked about life and eventually about the after-life. I looked at his sad eyes and I saw hopelessness. He asked me about the hope that I have. I explained to him the gospel of Jesus Christ. By the guidance of the Holy Spirit he surrendered his life right there. After I prayed with him he smiled and happily told me that he wanted to attend church if he ever got the chance to get out of the hospital alive. I visited him the next day and gave him a Bible. Just like all the others that I have had the privilege to lead to the saving faith of the Lord Jesus, I do not know where he is right now. My best hope is to see all of them someday in the presence of God.

Believers are blessed in many ways in order to be a blessing to others,

"and you will know the truth, and the truth will set you free" *John 8:32 (ESV)*

The veil of unbelief was removed from our eyes so that we can be instruments for others to find freedom. My hope for those who have become believers is that they will share the hope that is in them. My fervent prayer is that the Holy Spirit will touch the hearts and open the minds of those who do not know Jesus Christ and that they will eventually surrender to Him. May they realize that the time to do that is NOW.

I'm just grateful and blessed to have been used by God in furthering His kingdom.

"Not that I have already obtained this or am already perfect, but I press on to make it my own, because Christ Jesus has made me his own." *Philippians 3:12 (ESV)*

In a very inspiring speech of Denzel Washington he said, *"Put God first...I was directed, corrected, and protected. Everything that I achieved is all by God's grace."*

By the grace of God, along with fellow believers, we press on! The worst place to be on this side of eternity is to be outside of God's will. The worst of the worst that can happen in future eternity is for one to be outside of God's presence. Eternity is a long time!

•••••

Thorn Among the Roses. My former co-workers in Toronto while working as a Patient Care Assistant. (2012-2016)

With Rodge Gatilao, a Registered Nurse and now working as an Operating Room Nurse in Ottawa.

My former co-workers in Chicago, Illinois.

My Co-Workers in Aurora, Illinois. (L-R) Student Nurse, myself, Donna, Jamie, and Jon.

My Reliable Buddies. Security staff that respond during emergency situations. (L-R) Brittany, myself, Darin, Aron, Will, and Juan

(L-R) Jon, Darin, myself, Will, and Brittany

CHAPTER 13

THE GREATEST RESCUE OF ALL TIME

"For God did not send his Son into the world
to condemn the world, but that the world should be
saved through him."

— John 3:17 (NET Bible)

A lot of people would like to experience fun adventures like hiking, mountain biking, or surfing. Several people would like to participate in more challenging activities like bungee jumping or rock climbing. Only a few would actually dare to be a part of risky endeavors like joining the police force or the armed forces.

Of the few who dared, fewer still signed up to be a part of the elite fighting units. Those who do are a rare breed of men who have extraordinary fortitude. They are willing to offer their lives so that others may live in freedom and peace. There are only two persons who are willing to give up their lives for others: the soldier, to give others physical freedom; and God, who through Jesus Christ, offers those who come to Him eternal life.

Daring Rescues

Learning about daring raids and rescues in modern warfare is very interesting. One of the greatest known military rescues ever done was "The Raid at Entebbe" in Uganda, dubbed as "Operation Thunderbolt." It was a counter-terrorist hostage rescue mission carried out by the commando unit Sayeret Matkal of the Israel Defense Forces (IDF) at Entebbe Airport in Uganda in July 4, 1976.

The mission lasted for 90 minutes. It was conducted by 100 commandos who were airlifted from Israel and travelled for 4,000 kilometers or 2,500 miles to Uganda aboard four Lockheed C-130 Hercules aircraft. Information to IDF was provided by the Mossad, the national intelligence agency of Israel. Out of 106 hostages, 102 of them were rescued. Five Israeli commandos were wounded and killed in action was their commander, Lt Col Yonatan Netanyahu, a Harvard-educated professional and the older brother of Israel's Prime Minister Netanyahu.

All seven hijackers and 45 Ugandan soldiers were killed. Eleven Soviet-made MIG-1s and MIG-21s of Uganda's air force were destroyed. At this time, nothing of that magnitude has ever come close to that daring military operation.

In the Bible, particularly in *Genesis 14:5-7,* the four Mesopotamian kings attacked the rebellious cities in Canaan. Lot, Abraham's nephew (14:11-12) was taken captive. Abraham led the 318 trained men in a night raid akin to the method that elite units like the Scout Rangers are using nowadays. He brought about the victory in two ways: (1) He created maximum confusion to the enemy, and (2) He organized a divided force attacking from several directions, something we call Main Effort (ME) and Supporting Effort (SE) in modern military terms. The result was a blitzkrieg attack that scared the enemy into fleeing for their lives. They pursued them for over 150 miles towards the north of Damascus. It was a complete victory. In verse 16 (ESV), it says,

> "Then he brought back all the possessions, and also brought back his kinsman Lot with his possessions, and the women and the people."

Both of the sterling military achievements aforementioned by the Israelis and in biblical times by the Hebrews were only possible through Divine Providence. A diligent student of the Bible would surely be familiar with how God works His purposes through his chosen people. These two extraordinary rescue missions were done through human hands and efforts.

However, the greatest rescue of all time was not done by human beings but by the Creator of humankind. Rescue missions happen because there are captives. Captives do not have the ability to free themselves. They are subjected to the power of their captors. In order for captives to be freed, they need a Savior!

In the Raid at Entebbe, the hostages (Israelis) were captives of the hijackers (Palestinian terrorists) and the Ugandan military. They needed the Israeli commandos to save them because they did not have the power to save themselves from captivity. Likewise, Lot and his household needed Abraham and his trained men to save them from the Mesopotamian army.

Humankind is captive to sin and the devious schemes of Satan. The story of the "Fall of Man" can be found in *Genesis 3*. God planned the ultimate rescue mission. But in the meantime, the wickedness of man came to the point that God decided to wipe out humankind off from the face of the earth through a flood. But because God is gracious, merciful and just, He chose to preserve humankind through Noah, his sons, and their wives. *Genesis 6:9-9:17* narrates the story of Noah and the ark. In *Genesis 7:24 (NIV),* it says,

> "The waters flooded the earth for a hundred and fifty days."

God made a covenant with Noah and the sign is the appearance of the rainbow. In *Genesis 9:14-15 (NIV),* God said,

> "Whenever I bring clouds over the earth and the rainbow appears in the clouds, I will remember my covenant between me and you and all living creatures of every kind. Never again will the waters become a flood to destroy all life."

This is called the Noahic covenant.

After the flood, man multiplied and scattered over the face of the earth. But as they multiplied, their sins multiplied as well. In time, man built the Tower of Babel. This story is found in *Genesis 11:8-9 (NIV),* where it says,

> "So the Lord scattered them from there over all the earth, and they stopped building the city. That is why it was called Babel – because there the Lord confused the language of the whole world. From there the Lord scattered them over the face of the whole earth."

The Call of Abram (later named Abraham) found in *Genesis 12* is a crucial story to the faith we have today. God promised him a seed, land, and blessings. The seed was through his son Isaac, the land is Canaan, and the blessing is the faith we have today. The unilateral covenant was recorded in *Genesis 15*. It is called the Abrahamic covenant. *Galatians 3:7 (NIV)* says,

> "Understand, then, that those who have faith are children of Abraham."

God's Plan Prevails

The Messiah would come through the line of Abraham, so Satan tried his best to thwart God's rescue plan by disrupting that Jewish lineage. Satan operated through Pharaoh, who killed all male babies during the time of Moses. But through God's power, Moses was preserved and led the Hebrews out of Egypt. Their deliverance was completed when they crossed the Red Sea *(Exodus 14)*.

Satan's evil purposes were also evident during the time of the birth of Jesus, when King Herod ordered the killing of all newly born babies aged two years old and below after the Magi from the east informed him of the Messiah's birth *(Matthew 2)*.

God's sovereignty was and is always evident. Despite the diaspora that happened as a result of the Jewish captivity by the Assyrians (722 BC) and Babylonians (587 BC), the Jewish line that the Messiah would come from was preserved. In the fullness of time, the Messiah was born in Bethlehem as prophesied by Micah *(Micah 5:2)*. It was also prophesied in the 8th century BC by the prophet Isaiah. *Isaiah 9:6 (NIV)* says,

> "For to us a child is born, to us a son is given, and the government will be upon his shoulders. And he will be called Wonderful Counselor, Mighty God, Everlasting Father, Prince of Peace."

Not only was His birth prophesied, but also His death. In *Isaiah 53:5 (NIV)* it says,

> "But he was pierced for our transgressions, he was crushed for our iniquities; the punishment that brought us peace was on him, and by his wounds we are healed."

The way that God rescued mankind by sending His son Jesus to die on the cross is strange and has been unacceptable to the Jewish people at that time and to other skeptics ever since. The title of one of John MacArthur's books says it well, "Hard To Believe" (2003).

Always Share the Grace

While working as a Patient Care Assistant in Toronto years ago, I happened to take care of a very wealthy and learned 96-year-old man. He was the former president of one of the prestigious universities in Canada. He was a scientist and was responsible for the invention and improvements of some significant health care machines. I earned his respect after several days of giving him tender loving care. His family liked me as well and we exchanged worldviews in our light moments. I tried to ask the man about the meaning of life and his concept of life after death. I was quite surprised with his answer, *"I have never really thought about those things, Oliver."* I don't judge him, but I was a bit perplexed. How could a person be so intelligent and yet somehow miss one of the most important questions in life? Then he asked me my thoughts on the issue. I hid my excitement as I used the opportunity to share my faith. He told me that it would be hard for him to believe that. He said he is a Jew by birth, but had never really practiced Jewish religious beliefs. I concluded that the truth about Jesus Christ cannot be understood by just sheer intelligence. It requires the Holy Spirit to quicken the spiritual deadness in a person in order to understand the things of God.

> "The person without the Spirit does not accept the things that come from the Spirit of God but considers them foolishness, and cannot understand them because they are discerned only through the Spirit." *1 Corinthians 2:14 (NIV)*

I could only do so much. Salvation is by God's grace through faith indeed.

At that time, the Jewish people expected a king who would deliver them from Roman oppression. From the world's perspective, nobody wanted a dead Savior. In the worldly context, who would ever want a rescuer crucified on the cross? What is amazing is that Jesus Christ arose from the dead after three days! He conquered death (*Mark 16, Luke 24*). *Luke 24:6* testifies, *"He has risen!"*

Jesus Christ is more than just a moral leader who lived and influenced the division of human history from Anno Domini (A.D.), a Medieval Latin phrase which means "in the year of the Lord", to Before Christ (B.C.) He is God incarnate. According to Lee Strobel, author of the book "The Case for Christ" (1998) that was later made into a movie in 2017, Jesus has a very bold claim. Either He is a lunatic or He is telling the truth. Jesus addressed His disciples in John 14:6 saying,

"I am the way and the truth and the life. No one comes to the Father except through me."

With this, He was exclusively claiming that He is God. You have the choice to believe.

Another thing that is necessary in a successful rescue is the willingness of the hostage to go with the rescuer, and not to remain with the captor. In the daring rescues that I mentioned, all of them would not have been completed if the Israeli hostages did not go with the rescuing commandos. Abraham would not have marched home as a victor had Lot and his household remained with their kidnappers. In the same manner, God has rescued mankind from sin but the sinner must repent.

Repentance is moving away from sin and going towards God. The sinner must accept God's offer of salvation and go with Him in order to complete the rescue. God's love is so immense that He does not want to drag people towards Him but instead allows them to exercise their free will. Man has to receive his free gift. The Greek word "Dorea," meaning free gift, particularly stresses on the gratuitous nature of the gift. This means it is something given above and beyond what is expected or deserved. We commonly call it Grace. It is the kind of gift Jesus offered to the Samaritan woman at the well (*John 4*), the prodigal son (*Luke 15*), and many more recipients all throughout the Scriptures.

The whole of humankind is captive to sin. *Romans 3:23 (NIV)* sums it up,

"For all have sinned and fall short of the glory of God"

Obviously, man cannot save himself from sin. Sin is something man cannot handle. It is in his flesh. People who rely on themselves alone cannot escape the devastating consequences of it. Sin is the main culprit in all our flaws, imperfections, and wickedness which further result in conflicts, war, and eventually physical death. *Roman 6:23 (NIV)* says,

"For the wages of sin is death."

•••

Humbly, I believe that God rescued me spiritually in order for me to lead the physical rescue of Gracia Burnham, so that in the future, she could be a powerful instrument used by God to rescue others from their sin. The rescue cost the death of Martin, which is tragic from all human angles. Gracia always mentions in her speeches that she never expected to be "the vessel". From our perspective, Martin would have been a better messenger, but God chose her for reasons beyond our human understanding.

My prayer after you read this book is that you will be rescued from your captivity – spiritual or otherwise. And if the Greatest Rescuer has rescued you already, my prayer for you is that you will be an instrument for others to also attain and experience spiritual freedom through Jesus Christ, the Ultimate King of kings and Lord of lords.

•••••

Family Reunion in the USA (July 2018)

My "extended family" during the Jurado Cup – USA, a gathering of Philippine Military Academy (PMA) alumni, associates and their families from around the world.

Blessed to be God's messenger for the New Life in Christ Fellowship Camp in Minnesota, USA. (August 2018)

Visiting Minnesota. (L-R) My PMA classmate James Acosta, his wife Romena, Ena and myself.

The Men of New Life in Christ Fellowship in Minnesota led by their good Shepherd Rev. Louie Santelices (seated second from the left).

Meeting my PMA classmate and province mate Dorlie Sayoco and his wife Tess in Minnesota

New Life in Christ Fellowship Church Camp (Hinckley, Minnesota)

Brothers in Christ in Minnesota. (Standing L-R) My PMA classmate James Acosta, Efren Malong, myself, Pastor Louie Santelices, Steve Tiongson. (Seated L-R) My fellow Scout Ranger Ryan Silva and Pastor Raymart Benihagan.

AFTERWORD

Before he found his true calling, former Scout Ranger officer Oliver Almonares often found himself in positions that would eventually make him one of the crucial players in Philippine military history. Although he never thought of himself this way, it cannot be denied that his name has earned a spot in the country's history books.

Ultimately, Oliver realized that he could give up everything as long as he had peace with the Lord. His journey towards spiritual salvation – through the horrors and scars of war and the challenges that he and his family faced as immigrants in another land — made everything worth it.

No matter what spot he finds himself in though, Oliver will always have a special place in his heart for his Scout Ranger brothers. They had bled with him after all in the numerous brutal battles they fought together over the years for God, country, and people.

Throughout his transformation from Scout Ranger to a man living a God-centered life, Oliver has also drawn strength from his wife, Maria Regina, or simply Ena to their family and friends. To her, Oliver has always been – first, foremost, and for always – a devoted husband and a good father to their daughter, Bea. She revealed this in her own words.

•••

Oliver and I met at West Visayas State University in 1987. We became classmates, good friends and eventually, special best friends. A military wedding took place in my hometown a year after he graduated from Philippine Military Academy, and immediately after he finished the Scout Ranger Course in 1996. Our daughter, Bea, came two years later.

Oliver comes from a Christian family and was raised in biblical upbringing. When I first met him, I did not have any idea that he was a Christian. It really did not show – he was loud and not soft-spoken, aggressive and not meek, overbearing and not humble as I perceive Christians should be. He was so different from his family members who are reserved, gentle, and modest. He went to a military academy and stayed that way. After he graduated and became a young lieutenant in 1995, he changed. He was louder, more combative, and annoyingly arrogant.

The first few years of our marriage were colorful – he would have some drinking sprees with his friends during vacation leaves, basketball brawls, and other "for the boys" stuff. As a husband, however, Oliver is perfectly the one for me. I love him, so I accepted everything about him. The same way he loves me with my flaws and all.

In early 2007, we started to go to Calvary Baptist Church located close to our home. He told me he had this inner longing for his first love, Jesus Christ. Oliver started to bring Bea to Sunday school in the same church. Through Sunday School classes, Bea understood the gospel and accepted Jesus Christ in her life. After regularly listening to sermons and testimonies, I was convicted of my sinfulness and need of a Savior. Later that year, I accepted Jesus Christ as my personal Lord and Savior.

I experienced what the Apostle Paul described in the Scriptures, particularly in 2 Corinthians 5:17 (NKJV), "Therefore, if anyone is in Christ, he is a new creation; old things have passed away; behold, all things have become new."

I learned to develop a special connection with God each day, and my journey as a Christian became more meaningful with Oliver as my walking Bible and personal spiritual counselor. In 2008, we decided to go to his family's church, Highlight Fundamental Baptist Church. I became more exposed to the Word of God by listening regularly to sermons and attending Bible studies. We also participated in conducting church activities like Vacation

Bible School (VBS), Women's Missionary Society (WOMISSO) Fellowships, Bible Basketball, and the music ministry. I gradually grew in the knowledge and grace of the Lord Jesus Christ through these church activities.

For once in my life, I made the right decision – that is, marrying Oliver, who became an instrument for me to know my Lord and Savior. As Bea and I develop our relationship with the Lord Jesus Christ, Oliver serves Him with unbelievable passion.

The person I knew back then who was loud, aggressive, and arrogant had undergone a total transformation. He always makes time to read and study the Bible with us, listen to sermons of various ministers, attend Bible studies and Sunday services, and join men's group sessions and conferences.

Oliver stopped his earthly vices. His PTSD attacks caused by his military experiences also stopped. Thanks to the healing power of the Holy Spirit! Moreover, I have not heard of any "boxing" incidents at basketball courts anymore. Surprisingly, he made the effort to get in touch personally with everyone he had physically or verbally offended and asked for forgiveness. For those he could not reach personally, he connected with them through Facebook messenger and asked for forgiveness. That is what I call humility! And who could possibly make him do that – only Jesus Christ through the Holy Spirit!

As a Christian family, we are not problem-free. We will continue to have trials as we strengthen our faith and with all humility depend entirely on God for wisdom, provision, and protection.

I love Oliver for the person he was the day I married him. I love him more now for the person he has become. I am looking forward to witness what God will do through him to give Him honor and glory. As his lifetime partner and best friend, I will be with him in this wonderful journey as we press on through God's amazing grace.

I am forever grateful that God gave Oliver to us to be an instrument for us to know Jesus Christ as our personal Lord and Savior, who will be with us for all eternity.

Ena

Grateful and blessed to have the gift of family.

MANDIRIGMA*

Ranger Oliver Almonares
Ranger Tony Bacus
Ranger Arturo Daquilenea
Ranger Cerilo Jagmoc
Ranger Reynaldo Cuevas
Ranger Pepito Cabalhin
Ranger Edwin Aguinaldo
Ranger Antonio Relao
Ranger Raul Colanta
Ranger Joel Gallardo
Ranger Ferdinand Maramag
Ranger Carlos San Pedro
Ranger Joel Dela Fuente
Ranger Domingo Abrahan
Ranger Radney Magbanua
Ranger Virgilio Villacorta
Ranger Oliver Combalicer
Ranger Angelito Echare
Ranger Elmo Colorado
Ranger Neal Salaum
Ranger Floro Lozano
Ranger Joel Babaran
Ranger Edwin Ogoy
Ranger Armando Batalla
Ranger Redante Maranan
Ranger Reymond Lachica
Ranger Sally Albao
Ranger Adrian Garcia
Ranger Eusebio Mangaso

Ranger John Andrada
Ranger Daniel Dang-il
Ranger Cesar Acosta
Ranger Arturo Bionson
Ranger William Bustinera
Ranger Valentino Losaria
Ranger Abelardo Fabros
Ranger Venancio Tagsip Jr.
Ranger Renato Meniel
Ranger Cris Ibugan
Ranger Rodelio Morales
Ranger Victor Gulocino
Ranger Carlito San Pablo
Ranger Isagani Villasis
Ranger Fredie Saplala
Ranger Kenneth Ababao
Ranger Melvin Dela Peña
Ranger Nelson Alquiza
Ranger Ali Pinoy
Ranger Wilson Vertudez
Ranger Ferdinand Tonga
Ranger Lito Maramba
Ranger Rizal Manimtim
Ranger Dennis Bugayong
Ranger Joseph Tanay
Ranger Nilo Marcelino
Ranger Abner Eustaquio
Ranger Evinson De Guzman
Ranger Joel Balasa

Ranger Jojit Navarra

Ranger Charlie Solomon

Ranger David Cocjin

Ranger Christopher Flores

Ranger Rodel Rosario

Ranger Glen Tamayo

Ranger Rodelio Tuazon

Ranger Alvin Maddatu

Ranger Liby Pauya

Ranger Dante Polenzo

Ranger Reginald Aguirre

Ranger Marianito Bolante

Ranger Ameloden Ali

Ranger Rodolfo Papillera Jr.+

Ranger Glen Tamayo+

Ranger Roger Jaramillo

Ranger Joseph Reyes

Ranger Edelio Quimson

Ranger Jayson Avellano

Ranger Ronie Catague

Ranger Raymond Kilayco

Ranger Pinion Lim

Ranger Arnel Gamba

Ranger Rodel Placido

Ranger Wenie Constantino

Ranger Rodrigo Herrera

Ranger Julieto Eucogco

Ranger Rudy Bacyadan+

Ranger Danilo Cabical+

Ranger Alexander Tolentino+

*The Scout Rangers of 15th Scout Ranger (*Mandirigma*) Company who fought with Oliver in the many brutal battles they had from 2001 to 2003 during his stint as company commander.

+Killed-in-Action (KIA)

GLOSSARY

AFP, or Armed Forces of the Philippines.

ASG, or Abu Sayyaf Group

Balikatan, a Filipino word which means "shoulder-to-shoulder, is an annual U.S.-Philippine military training event focused on a variety of missions, including humanitarian assistance and disaster relief, counter terrorism, and other combined military operations.

Balikbayan is a Filipino word which means "Filipino expatriate"

Battalion is a ground force unit composed of a headquarters and headquarters company and three or more line companies or similar units.

CAA, or Civilian Armed Auxillary. They are civilians who volunteered to support regular AFP personnel, and with the primary goal of protecting their respective communities from lawless elements preying on them.

Call sign is a message or code broadcasted by radio to identify the person broadcasting the message.

Clearing is the act of ensuring that an area – usually a building or other structures – is free from danger.

Company is a military unit composed of 80 to 150 soldiers and usually commanded by a major or a captain.

DPA or "Deep Penetration Agent", embeds himself in enemy territory or with the enemy to perform intelligence-gathering tasks.

ESV is the "English Standard Version" of the Holy Bible.

FSRR, or First Scout Ranger Regiment.

HPFA, or "High-powered Firearm", refers to long gun or submachine gun that is normally issued to military and police.

IED, or Improvised Explosive Device.

KIA, or Killed-in-Action.

KJV, or the "King James Version" of the Holy Bible.

LOA, or Line of Advance, refers to the direction that is expected to be maintained.

LOD, or Line of Departure, is the starting position for an attack on enemy positions.

LOC, or Line of Contact, is the demarcation between any two armies. They could be warring or allied armies.

MEDEVAC, or Medical Evacuation, is done to those who are injured, wounded, or experiencing any medical condition that needs immediate attention.

MILF, or Moro Islamic Liberation Front, is currently considered the main Mindanao-based separatist group. Recently, they signed a peace deal with the Philippine government and is now positively working for peace and stability in Mindanao region.

MNLF, or Moro National Liberation Front, is a Mindanao-based separatist organization in the Philippines. It seeks an independent Islamic state or autonomous region for the Filipino Muslim minority in Mindanao region.

NASB is New American Standard Bible

NET refers to New English Translation of the Holy Bible

NIV, or the "New International Version" Inclusive Language Edition of the Holy Bible.

NKJV means New King James Version of the Holy Bible

NLT is New Living Translation of the Holy Bible

OCS refers to the Philippine Army's Officer Candidate School.

PHP is Philippine Peso

RPG, or rocket-propelled grenade, is a shoulder-fired anti-tank weapon system that fires rockets equipped with an explosive warhead. They are used against armored vehicles such as armored personnel carriers (APCs).

SOCOM, or the Special Operations Command of the Philippine Army. The First Scout Ranger Regiment is under this Command.

SRB, or Scout Ranger Battalion. The number, or strength, of the battalion is appended to acronym. For example, when referring to the 1st Scout Rnger Battalion then it's "1SRB."

SRC, or the Scout Ranger Company. The number of the unit is appended to the acronym. For example, when referring to the 2nd Scout Ranger (Venceremos) Company then it's "2SRC."

TCP, or Tactical Command Post, refers to the small mobile tactical command post from where the division commander directs the battle. It is located forward in the battle area and is staffed by selected assistants.

TTP, or Tactics, Techniques, and Procedures are processes, or methods, used in military operations.

USD is United States Dollar

WIA, or Wounded-in-Action.

REFERENCES

Abuza, Zachary. (2005). *Balik Terrorism: The   Return of the Abu Sayyaf.* Pennsylvania, USA: Strategic Studies Institute, US Army War College.

Armed Forces of the Philippines (AFP). *"The lone Ranger at the port."* AFP, 09 March 2015.   Retrieved from AFP.mil.ph.

Basa, Mick. *"After 18 years, Tagum soldier killed in Erap's all-out war gets hero's burial."* Rappler, 30 April 2018. Retrieved from Rappler.com.

Bayoran, Gilbert. *"Valor awardee assigned deputy head of 303rd IB."* Visayan Daily Star, 28 July 2014. Retrieved from VisayanDailyStar.com.

BBC. *"Philippines unrest: Who are the Abu Sayyaf group?"* BBC, 14 June 2016. Retrieved from BBC.com.

Bondoc, Jarius. *"Medal of Valor: A question of heroes."* The Philippine Star, 22 June 2005. Retrieved from Philstar.com.

Burnham, Gracia. *"About Gracia."* GraciaBurnham.org, undated. Retrieved from GraciaBurnham.org.

Cabunoc, Harold. *"Scout Rangers: The legend continues."* The Philippine Star, 26 November 2011. Retrieved from Philstar.com.

Cahill, Mark, *"One Thing You Can't Do In Heaven".* Oklahoma, USA: Genesis Publishing Group, 2004.

Cal, Ben. *"Operation Daybreak: The Inside Story."* Philippine News Agency (PNA), 08 to 10 July 2002. Retrieved from Istorya.net.

Cariño, Jorge. *"Why slain soldier received AFP's highest award."* ABS-CBN News Online, 20 December 2013. Retrieved from News.ABS-CBN.com.

Catanduanes Tribune. *"MSgt. Francisco Camacho finally honored: Medal of Valor awardee gets bust after 60 years."* Catanduanes Tribune, 15 August 2015. Retrieved from CatanduanesTribune.com.

Curato, Nicole. (2011). *"The road to Oakwood is paved with good intentions: The Oakwood Mutiny and the politics of recognition".* Philippine Sociological   Review, 59 (2011), pp. 23-48. Retrieved from jstor.org.

Fonbuena, Carmela. *"Living Heroes: 5 Filipino soldiers who won the Medal of Valor."* Rappler, 20 December 2017. Retrieved from Rappler.com.

GMA News Online. *"Timeline: July 27, 2003 Oakwood Mutiny."* GMA News Online, 09 April 2008. Retrieved from GMANetwork. com.

Gutierrez, Natashya. *"How an Army captain died saving his soldier's life in Marawi."* Rappler, 23 September 2017. Retrieved from Rappler. com.

Hill, Andrew E. & Walton, John H. "A Survey of the Old Testament." Grand Rapids, Michigan: Zondervan, 2009.

Jamieson, R., Fausset, A. R., & Brown, D. *"Commentary Critical and Explanatory on the Whole Bible".* Oak Harbor, WA: Logos Research Systems, Inc., 1997.

Lee-Brago, Pia. *"Gracia flies home today."* ThePhilippine Star, 10 June 2002. Retrieved from Philstar.com.

MacArthur, John. *"Hard To Believe".* Nashville, Tennessee: Thomas Nelson, Inc., 2003.

MacArthur, John. *"The MacArthur Study Bible, English Standard Version".* Wheaton, Illinois: Crossway, 2010.

Mananghaya, James. *"9 Oakwood soldiers to walk free."* The Philippine Star, 18 October 2006. Retrieved from Philstar.com.

Matthews, K. A. *"The New American Commentary, Genesis 11:27-50:26"*. Nashville, Tennessee: Broadman & Holman Publishers, 2005.

McCoy, Alfred. *"Closer than Brothers: Manhood at the Philippine Military Academy"*. Manila: Anvil Publishing Inc., 1999.

Pareño, Roel. *"Burnham's rescue from Abu meticulously planned – military."* The Philippine Star, 11 May 2003. Retrieved from Philstar. com.

Philippine Daily Inquirer. *"What went before: Oakwood Mutiny and Trillanes' 2nd try to oust Arroyo."* Philippine Daily Inquirer, 04 September 2018. Retrieved from Inquirer.net.

Philippine Military Academy. *"History, traditions, and general information."* PMA, [undated]. Retrieved from PMA.ph.

Romero, Alexis. *"AFP facing younger, more aggressive Abu Sayyaf."* The Philippine Star, 18 November 2014. Retrieved from Philstar.com.

Rydelnik, Michael & Vanlaningham, Michael. *"The Moody Bible Commentary."* Chicago, Illinois: Moody Publishers, 2014.

Schreiner, Thomas R. *"The King In His Beauty, A Biblical Theology of the Old and New Testaments"*. Grand Rapids, Michigan: Baker Academic, a division of Baker Publishing Group, 2013.

Sibirsky, Daniel. *"Exempt nurses."* South Florida Sun-Sentinel, 6 May 2007. Retrieved from Sun-Sentinel.com.

South China Morning Post (as cited in Stratfor Worldview, 1998). Stanford University. *"Mapping militant organizations: Abu Sayyaf."* Stanford University, 20 July 2015. Retrieved from Stanford.edu.

Stratfor Worldview. *"In Philippine terrorist leader killed – but is celebration premature?"* Stratfor Worldview, 21 December 1998. Retrieved from Worldview.Stratfor.com.

Strobell, Lee. *"The Case for Christ"*. Grand Rapids, Michigan: Zondervan, 1998.

The Economist. *"Estrada's risky strategy."* *The Economist,* 21 September 2000. Retrieved from Economist.com.

The Holy Bible: *English Standard Version.* Wheaton, IL: Crossway Bibles, 2016.

The Holy Bible: *King James Version, Electronic Edition of the 1900 Authorized Version.* Bellingham, WA: Logos Systems, Inc., 2009.

The Holy Bible: *The New International Version.* Grand Rapids, Michigan: Zondervan, 2011.

The Holy Bible: *New American Standard Bible: 1995 Update.* La Habra, CA: The Lockman Foundation, 1995.

The Holy Bible: *New King James Version.* Nashville, Tennessee: Thomas Nelson, 1982.

The Holy Bible: *New Living Translation.* Carol Stream, Illinois, Tyndale House Publishers, 2013.

The Lexham Analytical Lexicon to the Septuagint. Bellingham, WA, 2012.

The New English Translation Bible (NET Bible), First Edition. USA: Biblical Studies Press, 2005.

Warren, Rick. *"Purpose Driven Life: What on Earth Am I Here For?"* Grand Rapids, Michigan: Zondervan, 2002.

ACKNOWLEDGMENT

A lot of people encouraged me to write a book after the rescue on June 7, 2002. I simply shrugged it off because I never saw the need to write about it. *"What is the need for it? I was simply doing my job as a soldier,"* I used to tell myself whenever the topic was brought up to me.

But on October 23, 2017, a year after I moved to the United States from Canada, I attended a Voice of The Martyrs Conference in Indiana. A lot of amazing things transpired that day. Several attendees asked me to sign their copy of Gracia Burnham's book after she acknowledged me in front of an audience. One of these attendees introduced himself to me as a U.S. Army Ranger and told me, *"I would like you to sign your own book the next time we meet."* I don't remember his name, but I will never, ever forget his words.

Driving home after the conference, God put in my heart a desire to write a book to give Him honor and glory. The events of that day, and the statement made by a fellow Ranger in particular, led me to start scribbling my thoughts when I arrived home that evening.

This book would not have been possible without the wizardry of my co-author, editor, and publisher, Dr. Phil Fortuno, who aptly guided me with his literary skills, shared with me his scholarly expertise, and most of all, provided the means of production and promotion. God truly made Doc Phil's unscheduled visit to my home in Illinois, USA on the first week of November 2017 a great instrument for the completion and realization of this book.

Information, reference materials, and invaluable assistance came from the former members of the 15th Scout Ranger (*Mandirigma*) Company, specifically Rangers Rene Mabilog, Ronie Catague, and Abelardo Fabros, who provided the After Battle Report

(ABR) of the rescue operation and other necessary documents. I am indebted to Ranger Samuel Tayawa, a member of SR Class 131-97, a fellow warrior and brother in Christ, who provided crucial facts on various Scout Ranger classes; to my sister Dr. Helen Hofileña for her literary acumen, and sharing articles and pictures of mine she compiled for years; to Rev. Louie Santelices, MDiv. for his theological wisdom; and most importantly to Gracia Burnham, who not only significantly helped me validate the facts and figures mentioned in this book, but whose influence and story have immensely helped in shaping mine.

I am very grateful for the unconditional support of the Almonares family, particularly of my 92-year-old mother Virginia, my wife Ena and my daughter Bea, who is the real writer in the family. Above all, I would like to acknowledge God Almighty for giving me the ultimate reason to write, that is, to proclaim Jesus Christ as the Lord and Savior of mankind.

Oliver D. Almonares

It is said, "Every battle-scarred soldier has a part of him that will forever remain on the battlefield." Indeed, people like Oliver and me will always look back with reverence to where we once were, to the people whom we were with in our most trying moments, and to all our past activities in the military service. We will always reflect on them with utmost respect and fondness. There are just too many lessons to learn and memories to cherish – and even share to everyone.

When I visited Oliver and Ena in Illinois, USA on the first week of November 2017, I never had an inkling that the visit would someday produce a book – this book. Although we had chatted over cups of coffee until the wee hours of every night that I was in their house, we did not give much serious thoughts about writing and eventually publishing an actual book in the near future about Oliver's life, military exploits, and spiritual transformation. Perhaps the closest we had was for Oliver to send me "bullet notes" if, and whenever, he got the time to do it. There was no deadline, no agreed story flow or even a basic writing format – only "bullet notes". I was surprised when Oliver told me a few months after my visit that he had sent me several "bullet notes". Oliver had indeed taken the time to painstakingly jot down whatever he could remember from fifteen years earlier. He persevered! And so here it is, *"THE RESCUE: God's Amazing Grace"* – in the flesh, so to speak.

Gathering data, collating documents, completing pertinent pieces of information, and other materials for this project led us to seek assistance from colleagues and old buddies who were gracious enough to lend a hand to us. They did go the extra mile to find and give us what we needed for the book; and as much as we wanted to recognize them here, they politely declined and preferred to remain nameless. All they asked was to ensure this project become a reality to give tribute to all the troops who had gone before us, especially to those who had paid the ultimate sacrifice in the name of God, country and people. Hence, to all the quiet professionals and warrior-heroes, we humbly dedicate this project not only to you but to your families as well – you deserve all the honor and respect we can possibly muster. You are our heroes.

Likewise, I am profoundly thankful to my family and loved ones - especially to my parents, Lorenzo and Purita - from whom I draw immense and boundless inspiration. Without them, life would not have been easier for me while working on this project and many others. Again, this is for you!

Lastly, but most importantly, I am eternally grateful to the Lord Almighty for granting me the wisdom, material resources and physical strength to carry on and see this book into fruition. You are our ultimate and forever Commander-in-Chief.

Phil Fortuno, PhD

Made in the USA
Monee, IL
08 November 2021